THE MAN CODE

KEYS TO UNLOCKING A BALANCED LIFE

---

1   3   12   120   3000

DR. DENNIS SWANBERG
with RON SMITH

The quoted ideas expressed in this book (but not Scripture verses) are not, in all cases, exact quotations, as some have been edited for clarity and brevity. In all cases, the author has attempted to maintain the speaker's original intent. In some cases, quoted material for this book was obtained from secondary sources, primarily print media. While every effort was made to ensure the accuracy of these sources, the accuracy cannot be guaranteed. For additions, deletions, corrections, or clarifications in future editions of this text, please write ManCode Publishing.

Scripture quotations are taken from:

The Holy Bible, King James Version

The Holy Bible, New International Version (NIV) Copyright © 1973, 1978, 1984, by International Bible Society. Used by permission of Zondervan Publishing House. All rights reserved.

The Holy Bible, New King James Version (NKJV) Copyright © 1982 by Thomas Nelson, Inc. Used by permission.

The New American Standard Bible®, (NASB) Copyright © 1960, 1962, 1963, 1968, 1971, 1972, 1973, 1975, 1977, 1995 by The Lockman Foundation. Used by permission.

Holy Bible, New Living Translation, (NLT) Copyright © 1996. Used by permission of Tyndale House Publishers, Inc., Wheaton, Illinois 60189. All rights reserved.

The Message (MSG)- This edition issued by contractual arrangement with NavPress, a division of The Navigators, U.S.A. Originally published by NavPress in English as THE MESSAGE: The Bible in Contemporary Language copyright 2002-2003 by Eugene Peterson. All rights reserved.

New Century Version®. (NCV) Copyright © 1987, 1988, 1991 by Word Publishing, a division of Thomas Nelson, Inc. All rights reserved. Used by permission.

The Holman Christian Standard Bible™ (Holman CSB) Copyright © 1999, 2000, 2001 by Holman Bible Publishers. Used by permission.

Cover Design by Steelehouse
Page Layout by Bart Dawson

ISBN 978-1-60587-060-1

Printed in the United States of America

Swan's *ManCode* does it for me when it comes to faith and friends!

Willie Robertson (Duck Dynasty)

The ManCode is a great tool for men to take inventory of the key relationships in their everyday lives.

Dr. David Jeremiah

The ManCode is an easy-to-read and understand book for all men, but contained in this message is a powerful and life changing formula.

Rudy Niswanger, Center, Kansas City Chiefs (Retired)

This little book should be required reading for every man! I wish I had read it much earlier. It would have jump-started my spiritual life by 20 years. Every member of our staff and team will get a copy of it. Simply put, this book is AWESOME!

Jerry Moore (Head Coach of Appalachian State University,
Three-Time National Champion Football Team, Led ASU to greatest upset
in history of College Football—ASU defeated Michigan 09/04/2007)

The ManCode is a fresh word for men today. I love it because it is both biblical and challenging for men. If you are ready for spiritual adventure, climbing the mountain of greatness, get in this book and there is no telling what God may do with you. Read it. Buy it. Give it away. Men need this book today!

Dr. Ronnie W. Floyd (Senior Pastor, First Baptist of Springdale and
The Church at Pinnacle Hills, AR)

So much of what takes place in churches today is fine as far as it goes, but leaves many men cold and indifferent. There is a way to reach men and bring them to faith in Christ! Men need to take their place as followers of Jesus, and this book will certainly enhance that vital premise!

Dr. Dan Betzer (Pastor, First Assembly of God, Ft. Myers, FL)

All men young or old, long-time Christians or newly committed Christians will benefit from understanding the numbers in *The ManCode*.

Coach Dutch Schroeder (former Baseball Coach and Professor
at Baylor University)

At times, men have a tendency to distance themselves from any type of relationship that goes beyond the surface. *The ManCode* describes not only the importance of taking relationships to a deeper, more intimate level, but gives practical advice on how to be the man God intended us to be through those relationships.

Brian Cline (President of Pastor Appreciation Ministries)

The ManCode unlocks the secret for men experiencing the life God intended. In this simple yet profound book, you will discover the five relationships God intended for every man to develop. This book is a must-read for every man.

Dr. Robert Jeffress (Pastor, First Baptist Church, Dallas, TX)

I love this book because it goes right to the heart of where men are. *The ManCode* unlocks the code that will help men reconnect. It shows how God designed us to live, work, play, and love in the atmosphere of healthy relationships.

Bill Dye (Senior Pastor, North Monroe Baptist Church, Louisiana)

The ManCode helps every man crack the code for living life at full capacity. I recommend this book to all my friends and practice the principles in my personal life!

Dr. Michael D. Miller (President and Executive Publisher for NavPress.com)

The ManCode is a seemingly simple five-number set. But they have the potential to change the life of any man willing to spend the few hours it takes to read. Get ready to do some soul searching.

Troy Dungan (Chief Weather Anchor, retired, WFAA-TV, Dallas / Ft. Worth)

This book helps me understand why I chose my personal board of directors several years ago. My relationship with these men has helped me through my difficult days and taught me to celebrate my good ones. It is because of these relationships with my "3"as well as my relationship with my God, that I am a stronger Christian. In short there is a peace and fulfillment in my life that is impossible to explain unless you understand *The ManCode* and the power of that code.

George Dunklin (President Of Ducks Unlimited)

TABLE OF CONTENTS

A NOTE FROM RON SMITH

I n 2005, Dennis Swanberg and I sat down in a coffee shop at the Opryland Hotel in Nashville to discuss one of Dennis's ideas. Because I've been his manager for over a decade, and because Dennis had produced numerous videos, had hosted a cable TV show, and had written several books, this brainstorming session was nothing new. Over the years, Swan and I had talked about hundreds of concepts, but this one was different. When Dennis began to share his thoughts, I could see that he was gripped by a level of passion—a sense of excitement and possibility—like I had never seen before.

Now, Dennis Swanberg is a pastor at heart, but he is also a very funny man. He has a natural gift for comedy, a gift that he has dedicated to the Lord. So it's no surprise that over the past ten years, he has traveled the world over encouraging audiences with his humor and his insights. And because he remains a pastor first and foremost, Dennis's real purpose isn't hard to understand: Swan just wants to see people come to know the Lord. But it doesn't stop there. Dennis also has a second passion, a second obsession that drives him to bounce out of bed in the morning. That second passion is men's ministries, and Dennis is *serious* about it. Swan believes that when good men are drawn to the Christ, that when likeminded guys gather and reach out to one another and to their communities, miracles happen.

So on that day in Nashville, when Dennis began to describe a sequence of numbers that had been on his heart—

numbers that, by the way, had a special significance for men—I knew he was wrapping his mind (and his heart) around a very important idea. Swan told me that if men could simply understand a short string of numbers—and if men could learn to live by them—their lives would be changed forever. And Swan believed that if enough guys learned how to share these numbers, we would see a true change in our homes, in our churches, and in our culture. So I listened to Dennis for an hour or so, and I began to share his excitement. That's when a title jumped into my head: *The ManCode*. Dennis immediately agreed on that title, and we started working on the details.

Fast forward two years. By this time, Dennis and I had worked through the basics of The ManCode, and we were ready to get serious about pulling everything together in a book. So we partnered with our friend Criswell Freeman, and we started to get our thoughts on paper. This short book is the umpteenth rewrite of the original text. Initially, we wrote a book that came in at a whopping 280 pages, but that seemed, at least to us, to be overkill for most guys. So we tried several other versions, shortening the text each time. Finally, we decided that we wanted you, the reader, to experience something like that very first conversation we had at Opryland, something you could easily digest in a couple of hours. We pray that this little book truly offers you that opportunity, the opportunity to unlock a code that will change your life. And we hope we've written it in a quick, easy-to-read style that won't make your eyes glaze over.

We know The ManCode works because we've seen it over and over again. So don't be surprised if you see that The ManCode is already working in your life and in the lives of those around you. But I have to warn you: please don't read any further if you are not ready to see major changes in your life. The ManCode will challenge you in ways that you may not have been challenged before. The ManCode is simple, and it's easy to share, but it may not be quite so easy to implement, especially if you're a grizzled guy who's set in your ways. But once you understand how important these numbers are to you and your loved ones, I predict you'll buy into The ManCode and share it.

Are you man enough to learn and live The ManCode? I pray that you are!

I want to dedicate this book to my two sons,
Chase and Cole.
My prayer is that they will see "the code" lived out
in my life on a daily basis.

A NOTE FROM DENNIS SWANBERG

I t's a simple question but a tough one: Who's your best friend?

If you're like most guys, you may answer, "I've got lots of friends." But that answer may be a copout because, if you're like most men, you have an oversupply of skim-the-surface friendships and an undersupply of the genuine kind.

We men are *so* predictable: As a way of avoiding even *the remotest possibility* of intimacy, most of us are quick to form a complex web of surface-level relationships, an ever-expanding collection of "buddies." Yet we never manage to develop even one *really* close friendship, and it doesn't stop there. When it comes to the most important relationship of all, the relationship that each of us chooses to establish with God, most of us are quick *to avoid* intimacy in that relationship, too. And that's where The ManCode comes in.

This book is about forming real (translation: intimate) relationships, starting with your relationship with the Creator of the universe and branching out from there. So The ManCode identifies an ever-expanding circle of connections, signified by this short string of numbers:

$$1 \qquad 3 \qquad 12 \qquad 120 \qquad 3000$$

The ManCode is deceptively simple, but I'm convinced that it can be a powerful tool for you, a way to reorganize your thoughts and revolutionize your life. I believe that if you can master the relationships that are represented by these five numbers, you'll establish the right priorities, make the right plans, diagnose any unforeseen difficulties, make midcourse corrections, and achieve the kind of positive results that you desire and God intends.

So prepare to unlock a combination that never fails. We call it The ManCode, and we're confident that it's God's special code *for you*.

I want to dedicate this book to my two sons,
Chad and Dusty and The Boys on The Bayou.

INTRODUCTION

During World War II, both sides encrypted their messages, and for good reason. Success on the battlefield depended upon surprise attacks, which meant that neither side wanted the other to know what was in the plans.

Thankfully, our side was able to break the enemy's code first, so we knew exactly where the bad guys were headed and what they were up to. Military historians estimate that our code breakers shortened the war by several years and saved millions of lives. In short, those who broke the code won the war . . . and the same applies to you.

If you want to win your own personal struggles against the enemies of hopelessness, failure, and temptation, you need to break the code for successful living, and you need to break it now. This book offers you that code.

By gaining a clear understanding of the elements that comprise The ManCode—and by putting those principles into practice—you'll be prepared to win the personal battles that you face every day: battles of the heart; battles of the mind; battles in your world, in your workplace, and in your home. You already know how tough those struggles can be, and you know how important it is to win them. But don't worry: If you use the right tools—and if you have the right code—like the U.S. military in World War II, you're destined for victory.

THE MAN
CODE

1   3   12   120   3000

Here's a simple code that can change your life. It's a series of numbers called The ManCode—five numbers that describe the crucial relationships you need to unlock your potential and achieve *real* success.

If you're a man who's leading a nearly perfect existence, a life free of foul-ups, bloopers, and blunders—and if you're clearly at peace with your path and your faith—then you've already cracked the code. And you're already reaping the rewards. But if you're like the rest of us, struggling from one day to the next, trying to do the right thing but often falling short (or down), then you need The ManCode, and you need it *today.*

To help visualize the code, think back on your teenage years. Remember the combination lock on your high school locker? And do you remember how you needed the right numbers in the proper sequence—the code—in order to get inside? If you spun the lock's dial in just the right way, click! The tumblers fell into place, the lock opened, and you were in business. Likewise, every man has a combination of numbers that, when applied in the proper order, can unlock his potential and revolutionize his life. This book is about you finding that combination and using it to discover who you are, where you're going, and what you're supposed to do when you get there.

Most men haven't come close to unlocking their own personal codes—they are still hanging out in the same old places, dealing with the same old issues, making the same old mistakes, suffering with the same old results, and living with the same old regrets that have kept them tied up in knots for years. To make matters worse, far too many guys aren't really at peace with their own particular situations: They believe, quite correctly, that they could be contributing more to the world, and they'd like to receive more in return for their contributions—but they're not sure how to get there from here.

If you're such a man, if you're a guy who's still got lots of room (and lots of desire) for improvement, here's the combination—we've chosen to call it The ManCode—a string of five numbers that will unlock a world of opportunities for you:

1   3   12   120   3000

What do these numbers mean? To get things started, let's take a minute and consider each part of The ManCode:

1

The first number of The ManCode is **1**. It signifies your need for a One-to-one relationship with God. This is the most important number in your Code, and it is non-negotiable. This number of The ManCode, like the Being it describes, does not change—not today, not tomorrow, not ever.

Face it: You're hardwired for a relationship with something bigger than yourself. If you don't have it, that's why you're empty. If you don't have it, that's why you're miserable when it gets quiet—you can't stand to be alone with yourself because you weren't created to be alone. Whether you realize it or not, you possess a deep desire to experience a One-to-one connection with the Creator of the universe. God made you that way; it's simply part of who you are; it's woven into your DNA. *But . . .*

If you're like most men, you discovered a long time ago that finding *lasting* fellowship with the Creator isn't easy. Why? Because you're not only wired up to *need* a relationship with God, but you're also hardwired to want things your own way. That means you're constantly tempted to *resist* God and to *rebel* against His laws (think about man's fall in the Garden of Eden). You're probably just a little too hardheaded—and you're probably just a little too fond of instant gratification—for your own good. As a result, you probably have a tough time when it comes to the difficult job of obeying your Heavenly Father. And you're not alone. Everybody resists God at one time or another, and so will you. But as you mature, you should realize that when it comes to God's instructions, it's better to be teachable than headstrong.

Great athletes can be successful, at least for a while, with nothing more than raw talent. But in order to win consistently at the highest levels of competition, even the best players need great coaches. God is the ultimate Coach—are you coachable? Are you willing to listen to your Heavenly Father and learn from Him, or do you insist on doing things "your way"?

To crack The ManCode, you've got to decide who's in charge: It's either you or God. Only you can determine whether you'll pay attention to the Coach, or not. Only you can decide whether you'll be a teachable man, or a stubborn know-it-all. Only you can choose to be a team player on *God's* team, or not. But of this you can be sure: If you want to be a winner in the truest sense of the word, you'll need to let God call the plays, which means you'll need to build a One-to-one relationship with Him. And that means letting God call the signals on every down.

3

The second number of The ManCode is **3**, a number that signifies three friends you can trust completely. This number is negotiable: For you, the number might be 2, it might be 3, or it might be 4. But whatever the exact number is for you, please keep the group small, and please make sure that these guys are Christian men who will be there for you in good times and bad.

Every man needs a small group of Christian friends, a cadre of trusted counselors to watch his back, to hold him accountable, and to carry him when he can't carry himself. If there's a problem, these guys are available 24-7, no questions asked. But most men aren't comfortable with *really* close relationships like this. If you're one of those guys, get over it.

New Testament scholars point out that Jesus seems to have forged special relationships with three disciples: Peter,

James, and John. These three men appear to have formed Christ's inner circle. What was good for Jesus is good for you, too . . . only more so. After all, Jesus was the Son of God; He was accountable only to the Father. But you're accountable to a wide range of people: family, friends, and coworkers, for starters.

In the last several years, the word *accountability* has become very popular in Christian circles. But like everything else that we humans get our hands on, we've managed to trivialize its meaning and water it down. Please don't make that mistake. If you want to be a real success, make up your mind to hold yourself—and your closest confidants—accountable in the truest sense of the word.

The dictionary defines *accountability* as "the act of making a person responsible for his actions." And that's exactly what your "group of **3**" should do for you. These three men should help you take inventory of your life: your victories and defeats, your strengths and shortcomings, your big plays and your boneheaded blunders. And you should do the same for them. To have a **3**, you must be a **3**.

So even if you consider yourself a loner, remember that you still need a small group of high-octane comrades-in-arms—men who are as close to you as brothers, men who are firmly grounded in their relationship to God. These are the guys who know almost everything about you but love you anyway.

Real friendship between men, the kind of right-down-there-in-the-foxhole-with-you mentality that we're describing here, is far less common than you might think because most of us guys are more comfortable with surface-only friendships. We want to appear large-and-in-charge, so we never really express our deepest emotions to other men, not even to our closest friends. That's why most guys have lots of acquaintances but very few *really* close friends. And this causes big problems because all men (including you) need allies that are totally trustworthy, totally available, and totally supportive.

In selecting your own group of **3**, you should look for guys who will *always* tell you the truth, no sugarcoating allowed. They should be men who are courageous enough to call you on the carpet when appropriate. They should know how to pump you up (when you're down) and how to celebrate your victories (when you're up). Your group of **3** should be willing and able to help you handle your frustrations, your hurts, and your humiliations. And these guys can also serve as emotional trash collectors by helping you dispose of any mental garbage you've managed to accumulate. These buddies are always on call, and your secrets are always safe with these rugged saints.

12

The next number in The ManCode is **12**, a number, by the way, that appears over and over again in the Bible. So if you were raised in and around a church, the number **12** should come as no surprise. When Jesus was looking for companions to share the load of His ministry, He chose a dozen men. And even *after* Christ ascended, the disciples quickly gathered and elected a twelfth man to take Judas' place.

In The ManCode, **12** is a negotiable number. Perhaps your "large group" will be numbered in single digits, or maybe you'll have more than a dozen. The exact number isn't crucial, but the group itself *is* crucial. Even Jesus felt it was important to have a group of men to eat with, to fellowship with, and to travel with—and since it was good enough for Him, it's good enough for you, too.

This "group of **12**" is a larger collection of friends and supporters. Many, but not necessarily all, will share your Christian faith (by the way, if you're worried about hanging out with non-Christians, remember that Jesus made Himself available to saints and sinners alike—and if you're serious about leading non-believers to Christ, you probably can't do it while preaching to the choir).

The **12** men who make up your larger group should be guys whose company you enjoy. They're guys you can golf with, fish with, travel with, and worship with. They offer friendship and fellowship, but it shouldn't stop there. You can also think of your group of **12** as a launching pad to the world, a dozen men who possess a diversity of experiences, opinions, and contacts. By using this larger group as a source of inspiration, information, and support, you can climb the ladder of success much faster and much farther than you could if you were climbing solo. But make no mistake: the relationships you form in your group of **12** will be of little use to you *until* you have the numbers 1 and 3 firmly in place. It's back to the example of your high school lock combination: first 1, then 3, and then **12**.

But there's more.

TWO MORE NUMBERS: 120 AND 3000

The number **120** stands for the church. You may attend a church that's much larger or significantly smaller than that, which is perfectly okay. But we've chosen the number **120** for a very good reason: In the Book of Acts, we are told that on the day before Pentecost about **120** believers gathered in an upper room in Jerusalem. This band of believers gave a jumpstart to the early church—and your participation in a local church can help jumpstart your world, too.

Now you may be thinking, "Here we go again; another push to get me to go to church." And if you're thinking that, you're right. You need the church much more than the church needs you. And you need it right now!

The local church is at the heart of God's plan for *our* world *and* for *your* world. The church has all the spiritual gifts, human skills, and earthly tools it needs to accomplish God's will, so if you're serious about involving yourself in His master plan, you need to do so by throwing yourself into the work of His church.

In 1 Corinthians 3:16, Paul states that we believers *are* the church, but too many of us aren't behaving like it. Instead, too many of us (especially us *guys*) are watering down the importance of corporate worship. But God has other intentions. He wants us to share Christ's message in church, and He wants us to show the world how our lives have been changed because of our relationship with His Son.

By the way, have you noticed the progression from 1 to 3 to 12 to **120**? And can you understand how that progression might work for you? You begin with a One-to-one relationship with God. Then, you expand your influence by finding (and keeping) three trusted friends, men who are rock-solid brothers in the faith. Next, you increase your influence with a robust group of buddies numbering about a dozen (or more). And then, as an active member of a church, you experience yet another multiplier effect. And that's where the number **3000** comes in.

The last number of The ManCode is **3000**. It's the number of men and women who responded to Peter's invitation to be baptized on the day of Pentecost, so this number signifies the need to reach out to your community and to the world. It's a number that reminds us of the miraculous things that can occur when God works in the lives and hearts of His children and His churches.

Think of all the things that came after the Pentecost: churches were built, fellowships were established among believers, mission trips were launched, lives were forever changed, and the Good News was spread far and wide. The echoes of those great victories are still heard around the world today.

THINK ABOUT YOUR OWN CODE

Throughout this book, you'll be asked quite a few questions, all of which are intended to help you crystallize your thoughts and formalize your own personal Code. You'll be asked to identify the names of the men in your group of 3 and in your group of 12. Plus, you'll be asked some straightforward questions about your life, your path, your passion, and your faith.

If you're up to the challenge, it's time to turn the page and get started. And the best place to begin, of course, is at the Beginning (with a capital *B*) which, not surprisingly, is **1**.

1   3   12   120   3000

GOD DOESN'T WANT YOUR ABILITY— HE WANTS YOUR AVAILABILITY.

———

Bobby Bowden

Think, for a moment, about the difference between wants and needs. When you *want* something (you know *that* feeling), you have an *urge* to go after it. And if you're like most guys, you won't stop until you get it. But *needs* are very different from wants. You can ignore the things you *need* for years, for decades, or even for a lifetime—and scarcely notice what you've been missing.

For example, you *need* a healthy diet, but you may not want it. And you *need* about eight hours sleep every night, but you may not get it. You *need* to focus on your family and your future; but left to your own resources you may be tempted to focus, instead, on beer, bad habits, babes, and barbecue.

Life would be much easier if your wants and needs were always the same, but it doesn't work that way. All too often, the things you *want* you don't *need*, and the things you *need*, you simply don't *want*.

You'll go through periods when your wants take center stage and your needs are relegated to the nosebleed seats. During these times, your wants can take control of your life, leaving little time and energy for your real needs. So if you haven't been feeling a very big need for God lately, it's possible that your long list of wants may be crowding out your need for God. But the good news is this: The minute you face up to your need for the Father, He responds. God is not hiding out and He's not on vacation, so you can always find the Creator *if* you make up your mind to look for Him.

God is wherever you happen to be. He's with you every moment, and He wants to be a full partner in every aspect of your life. That's why The ManCode begins at the very same place your life should begin: *with God.*

If you're totally committed to a One-to-one relationship with your Creator—if you're wise enough to make God the first page on your life's playbook—you're already destined to be a winner. After all, God has a far better perspective than you. So if you're willing to let the Creator call His plays from the press box (while you refrain from the temptation to call your own audibles from the line of scrimmage), you'll be victorious.

But if you stubbornly insist on calling your own plays on every snap, you're destined for a losing season. In other words, if you attempt to carve out parts of your life that are separate from God—if you're trying to have a relationship with the Father on Sunday morning while ignoring Him the rest of the week—you're setting yourself up for defeat. So remember that God is talking directly to you when He says, "My thoughts are not your thoughts, nor are your ways My ways. For as the heavens are higher than the earth, so are My ways higher than your ways, and My thoughts than your thoughts" (Isaiah 55:8-9 NKJV).

God must do everything for us.
Our part is to yield and trust.

A. W. Tozer

Commandment #1 Says That God Is #1

The first of the Ten Commandments leaves
no room for interpretation:

Thou shalt have no other gods before me.

Exodus 20:3 KJV

The story of the Ten Commandments appears
twice in the Old Testament, in Exodus (Chapter 20)
and in Deuteronomy (Chapter 5). When God decided
to inscribe His words on those stone tablets, He didn't
intend for them to be "The Ten Suggestions." Nope,
God meant *exactly* what He said. When God gave His
ten laws to Moses on Mt. Sinai, the Father meant for
His commandments to be obeyed, with no exceptions,
starting with commandment #1, which clearly states
that God comes first and everything else comes next.

SOCIETY ENCOURAGES YOU TO IGNORE GOD

You live in a society that encourages you to relegate
God to a few hours on Sunday morning, or to ignore Him
altogether. You're part of a culture that encourages you to
treat God's laws as mere recommendations, to be accepted
or rejected based upon your own particular circumstances or

your own particular desires. And, you live in a society that tempts you to think of yourself first, yourself second, yourself third, and God last. That's why it's no surprise that society is so thoroughly confused: Society looks to itself for guidance not to the Creator.

To further complicate matters, you inhabit a world in which a near-infinite number of distractions threaten to gobble up your moments, your days, and your life. Every day you face temptations that are more numerous—and more dangerous—than ever. You're bombarded with messages that claim you can find (or more accurately "buy") happiness "out there" with a woman or at the car lot or in the luxury suite or at the local watering hole. All you've got to do, the world says, is to bet all your chips on the worldly stuff; and if you happen to acquire enough man-sized toys, you're set for life. Meanwhile, the world writes God out of the picture.

The great irony, of course, is that humanity already possesses everything it needs to acquire genuine peace and abundance. We've already been given clear directions for life here on earth and for life eternal; it's all spelled out in the Bible. But since most guys hate to ask for directions (even when those directions come straight from God), we sometimes refuse to use God's manual. So it's no wonder our lives get messed up—we just can't seem to make ourselves follow the right instructions. The Bible teaches us, "In all your ways acknowledge Him, and He shall direct your paths," (Proverbs 3:6 NKJV) but sometimes, in spite of ourselves, we choose the wrong path.

The world's messages are often subtle, encouraging you to do what "feels good" as long as nobody gets hurt, all the while encouraging you to distance yourself from your Maker. But if you distance yourself from the Creator, somebody *always* gets hurt, and that somebody is always *you*. And it doesn't necessarily stop there: other people are injured, too. Whenever you detach yourself from God, you'll inevitably— if unintentionally—inflict collateral damage on family members, on friends, and even on strangers. Yes, ignoring God is dangerous, but this message isn't getting through to large segments of society.

Society tells you that it's okay to go to church on Sunday—for appearance's sake—but that you're not really a man unless you de-focus on God and refocus on self and stuff throughout the rest of the week. So you're encouraged to write God out of your script as you invest everything you've got in the futile search for "happiness" as the world describes it. Yet the world gets it wrong: Real happiness doesn't come from indulging yourself. You can't find lasting happiness at the local watering hole or anyplace else where worldly pleasures are sold to the highest bidder. Genuine abundance comes only from God . . . and from His only begotten Son. When you establish a One-to-one relationship with God, you learn to live in the world but not to worship it. Yet it's tougher than ever to put God first because the world seems to cry, "Worship me with your time, your money, your energy, and your thoughts!" To resist these temptations, you need a One-to-one focus, a focus that requires genuine obedience, not lip service.

Society has written God out of many of our schools and public places, but you must never write Him out of your heart. Are you willing to place God first in your life? And are you willing to welcome God's Son into your heart? Unless you can honestly answer these questions with a resounding yes, then your relationship with God isn't what it could be or should be. Thankfully, God is always available, and He's waiting to hear from you now. In fact, He's calling to you right now, just like He called out to Adam: "Where art thou?" The answer to His calling, of course, is entirely up to you.

SOMETIMES, YOU MAY FIND YOURSELF WRESTLING WITH GOD

The man said, "Let me go; it's daybreak."
Jacob said, "I'm not letting you go 'til you bless me."
The man said, "What's your name?" He answered, "Jacob."
The man said, "But no longer. Your name is no longer Jacob.
From now on it's Israel (God-Wrestler);
you've wrestled with God and you've come through."

Genesis 32:26–28 MSG

In Genesis 32, we are told about Jacob's encounter with God. It was, quite simply, a wrestling match for the ages. Despite exhaustion, despite weariness, Jacob simply wouldn't let go. Even when God dislocated Jacob's hip, the determined man refused to quit. Even after wrestling all night, and even after daybreak, Jacob persevered until God finally agreed to bless him. God changed Jacob's name to Israel, which means "he struggles with God." Thus, Jacob formed a spiritual contract as a result of his struggle with—and against—the Creator.

Jacob wrestled with God, and so, at times, will you. Sometimes, you'll struggle to earn God's blessings, and just like Jacob, you'll soon discover that the struggle isn't easy. Jacob battled with God before he experienced God's blessing—and perhaps you, too, will grapple long and hard (by trying to do it *your* way, not God's way) before you finally decide to let God's rules become your rules. But the good news is this: When you decide, once and for all, to let God run things, you'll receive the big-time rewards that your Father has in store for you, the kind of rewards that really matter: *the eternal ones.*

It's worth noting that we human beings find it terribly difficult to view things from an eternal perspective. We want the kind of earthly rewards (fancy cars, big houses, you know the rest) that seem, at least to us, to be important. But God sees things differently. He wants us to focus on the important things: the spiritual rewards that last a lifetime. That's what He meant when He said, "Don't collect for yourselves treasures on earth, where moth and rust destroy and where thieves break in and steal. But collect for yourselves treasures in heaven, where neither moth nor rust destroys, and where thieves don't break in and steal. For where your treasure is, there your heart will be also" (Matthew 6:19-21 Holman CSB).

So you, like Jacob, should enter into a *spiritual* contract with your Creator, a rock-steady partnership that binds you to Him today, tomorrow, and for a lifetime. And as you hammer out the details of that partnership, you'll find that in order to receive God's blessings, you must be obedient to His will. And to be obedient to His will, you must try, as best you can, to figure out what He wants you to do with your life—you must follow wherever God leads, even if He leads you through some tough times.

God allows us to experience the low points of life
in order to teach us lessons
that we could learn in no other way.

C. S. Lewis

Mark it down: things do not "just happen."
There is a God-arranged plan for this world of ours,
which includes a specific plan for you.

Charles Swindoll

The "One" (with a capital *O*)
to "one" Relationship:

Throughout this book, we describe your relationship with God as *One-to-one*. The capital O, as you might imagine, refers to your Heavenly Father, while the lowercase *o* refers to you. This grammatical construction is deliberate: It's intended to remind you that God is God, and you're not (even though the world would have you believe it's the other way around).

SOMETIMES GOD KNOCKS YOU DOWN BECAUSE HE WANTS YOU TO BE A WINNER

Sometimes, God allows you to be knocked down by the consequences of your behavior (or, more accurately, misbehavior) *before* He lifts you up. He does so (surprisingly enough) because He loves you. He knows that when you obey Him you win, and when you disobey Him you lose—but *you* may not know that. So God may have to teach you things the hard way because the easy way simply isn't getting through. Sometimes, you must *get caught* in order to *be taught*.

It's like the old story of the farmer who smacked his stubborn mule with a 2x4. As the farmer was swinging from his heels, a passerby city-slicker asked, "Why are you beating your own mule?" The farmer replied, "It's the only way I can get his attention." And from time to time, God may have to treat you like that farmer treated his mule. During these tough times, it may feel like the Father has given you a whack on the side of the head, when, in reality, your own choices have caused the pain.

Did you ever have a high school coach who got into your face? If so, you remember that when you made a mistake, good ol' Coach got nose-to-nose with you, so close that you could smell the onions he had piled on his lunchroom cheeseburger. Why did Coach invade your space? The same reason that God needs to do it. Sometimes you need communication that's simply too clear to misinterpret. And because God has a program that never fails, He wants you to be a contributing member of the winning team.

Are you really listening to God? Are you willing to hear and learn? When God gets in your face, are you willing to pay attention? Well, if you want to experience His brand of success, that's exactly what you must do.

As We Get Older, We Appreciate the Tough Coaches Who Cared Enough to Set Clear Boundaries

When we're young, we tend *not* to appreciate the coaches and teachers who make us tow *their* line every step of the way. In fact, we may resent any authority figure who sets clear boundaries and establishes rock-solid expectations. But as we get older, we become more grateful for those rugged disciplinarians who cared enough to make us do our best.

God wants you to do your best, and He knows you can't succeed unless you tow *His* line. So if His discipline seems tough today, rest assured that He has bigger and better things in store for you tomorrow.

THE DOMINOS GUY DELIVERS MORE THAN PIZZAS

Tom Monaghan has formed a full-fledged partnership with God, and it's working out quite nicely, thank you very much. But success didn't come easy for the man who practically invented the pizza delivery business. You see, Tom's father died when Tom was only five, and his mother, who was a low-paid domestic worker, tried but failed to hold her family together. So young Tom bounced around from one foster home to another until he finally ended up in a Catholic orphanage, where he was forced to focus, at least for a while, on the Gospels.

Although the odds were stacked heavily against him—Tom finished dead last in his high school class—Monaghan wasn't a quitter. So with a hard-earned high school diploma in hand, he enlisted in the Marines, served his country, and mustered out with a few dollars, which he promptly invested—and lost—in a worthless oil deal.

But there was still a small ray of light at the end of Tom's tunnel because he and his brother had remained close, and his brother had managed to make a down payment on a tiny pizza shop in Ypsilanti, Michigan. So the two men became partners until Tom's brother found a better job working at the local post office. Then, in what may have been one of the best business deals of all time, Tom traded his used VW Beetle for his brother's half interest in the pizzeria. Now Tom had become the sole proprietor of Domino's Pizza.

By now you've probably figured out the rest of the story: Tom worked hundred-hour weeks, slaved over a hot pizza oven, franchised his pizza restaurants, and made a fortune. And to make up for the things he didn't have as a kid, he bought just about everything in sight, including jets, helicopters, mansions, artwork, and even the Detroit Tigers. But none of those things filled the God-shaped hole at the center of Tom's heart. So the alpha-Domino-guy, remembering the lessons of his youth, finally put things in proper perspective and turned everything back over to God. Tom turned over his heart, his business, his money, and his life—he held nothing back from the Father.

Today, as one of America's biggest contributors to Christian causes, Tom Monaghan is reaching out and making a difference. Yet he's not overly impressed with money. He observed, "I had to get rich to see that being rich isn't important."

Monaghan's approach to money management is simple. He says, "Now I realize that it's God's money, not mine."

What *is* important to Tom—vitally important—is his One-to-one relationship with the Creator.

Can the same be said for you?

————————————

Jesus Christ is the first and last, author and finisher,
beginning and end, alpha and omega,
and by Him all other things hold together.
He must be first or nothing.
God never comes next!
Vance Havner

A FEW MAN-TO-MAN QUESTIONS FOR YOU

1. Tell the truth: Are you really comfortable about your relationship with God? Rate yourself by choosing the sentence below that best describes you:

   A. You're totally comfortable talking about your faith—or demonstrating it—in just about any situation.

   B. You're comfortable talking about your faith in safe settings (like in church or at home), but you're less likely to express those feelings in less secure settings (like in the workplace or at non-church public functions).

   C. Even when you're at home or at church, you still find it difficult, but not impossible, to talk about your relationship with God.

   D. You're so uncomfortable with your faith that you never talk to other people about it.

2. List three things that are currently as important (or more important) to you than your relationship with God.

   _____

   _____

   _____

   _____

3. Try to visualize what your life might be like if you had a closer relationship with God. Do you think that things would be better, worse, or about the same? Be specific: consider how a closer relationship with the Creator might impact your family, your job, your relationships, or your health.

_____

_____

_____

_____

_____

_____

_____

_____

_____

_____

_____

_____

_____

_____

_____

_____

BEFORE YOU MOVE ON . . .

*At the name of Jesus every knee should bow, of those in heaven,
and of those on earth, and of those under the earth,
and that every tongue should confess that Jesus Christ is Lord,
to the glory of God the Father.*

Philippians 2:10-11 NKJV

The Bible teaches us that Jesus is *the* bridge—not *a* bridge—to God. Period. The Bible makes it clear that at the name of Jesus every knee should bow and every voice should proclaim Him Savior. And the Bible instructs us time and again that a real relationship with Christ is *the* unique path, not only to earthly abundance but also to eternal life. Nonetheless, in some Christian circles, it has become fashionable to talk *lots* about God and *little* about His Son (meanwhile, the Holy Spirit is often ignored altogether). As strange as it might seem to previous generations of believers—or, for that matter, to the countless martyrs who sacrificed their lives rather than repudiate Jesus—some Christian writers have found it convenient (and quite popular) to focus on the concept of God while deemphasizing the other two parts of the Holy Trinity. We don't intend to make that mistake. We believe that the Bible means precisely what it says about God, about Jesus, and about the Holy Spirit.

So it's time to ask yourself the most important question of all: **Do you have a One-to-one relationship with Jesus?**

If you can genuinely answer this question with a resounding yes, feel free to move ahead to the next chapter. But, if you're uncertain or ambiguous about your relationship with Christ, please stop reading right now and take time to think about— and more importantly to pray about—your relationship with God and His Son.

Simply put, you need a life-altering, One-to-one relationship with Jesus. Jesus is the way, and there's no side entrance.

Period.

And if you don't yet have that relationship, here's how you can get it:

The Plan of Salvation

1. Understand that God loves you, and He demonstrated that love by sending His only begotten Son in order that you might have abundance and eternal life.

For God so loved the world, that he gave his only begotten Son, that whosoever believeth in him should not perish, but have everlasting life.

John 3:16 KJV

I am come that they might have life, and that they might have it more abundantly.

John 10:10 KJV

2. **Admit that you, like all human beings, have sinned. Sin separates you from God. A spiritual rebirth takes place when you turn your life over to Jesus Christ.**

For all have sinned and fall short of the glory of God.

Romans 3:23 Holman CSB

For the wages of sin is death, but the gift of God is eternal life in Christ Jesus our Lord.

Romans 6:23 Holman CSB

3. **Believe that salvation is made possible by Christ's death and resurrection.**

For Christ also suffered once for sins, the just for the unjust, that He might bring us to God, being put to death in the flesh but made alive by the Spirit.

1 Peter 3:18 NKJV

In Him we have redemption through His blood, the forgiveness of our trespasses, according to the riches of His grace that He lavished on us with all wisdom and understanding.

Ephesians 1:7-8 Holman CSB

4. Invite Christ to rule over your heart and your life. When you do, you will be "born again."

Therefore repent and turn back, that your sins may be wiped out.

Acts 3:19 Holman CSB

For by grace you are saved through faith, and this is not from yourselves; it is God's gift—not from works, so that no one can boast.

Ephesians 2:8-9 Holman CSB

5. If you accept what you have just read, pray the following prayer right now:

A Sinner's Prayer

Dear Jesus, I am a sinner. But, I believe that You died and rose from the grave so that I might have eternal life. Come into my heart, Jesus, take control of my life, forgive my sins, and save me. I am now placing my trust in You alone for my salvation, and I accept Your gift of eternal life. Amen

WHAT NEXT?

If you've just prayed the Sinner's Prayer—or if the ideas in this chapter have caused you to rearrange your priorities and your life—it's time to get up out of your chair and do something. Here are three things you can do:

1. **Let somebody else know what's happened**. Call at least one Christian friend, and let him know about the changes you've just experienced. In order to strengthen your faith, you need to talk about it. If you don't know another Christian, pray for guidance to reach out to a local pastor. And be watchful because God will lead you to someone who can help.

2. **Make up your mind to become a disciple *today* (because tomorrow may be too late).** Jesus doesn't want you to get with the plan some day; He wants you to follow Him today:

Then Jesus said to His disciples, "If anyone wants to come with Me, he must deny himself, take up his cross, and follow Me. For whoever wants to save his life will lose it, but whoever loses his life because of Me will find it."

Matthew 16:24-25 Holman CSB

3. **Get involved in a church**. In order to grow as a Christian, you need to surround yourself with other believers. But you don't have to become a member of the first church you visit. Take time to listen, to pray, to study Scripture, and to ask God to lead you to the right place of worship. He is faithful to lead you to where you should be.

———————————

Only participation in the full life of a local church builds spiritual muscle.

Rick Warren

3

1   3   12   120   3000

THE NEXT BEST THING
TO BEING WISE ONESELF IS
TO LIVE IN A CIRCLE OF
THOSE WHO ARE.

—

C. S. Lewis

The number **3** stands for your "small group," a trio of trustworthy men with whom you can share your thoughts, and who will watch your back and hold you accountable. These three guys form your inner circle; they are your most faithful allies and advisors.

The number **3** is negotiable, up to a point. You may have two, three, or four guys who make up your team, but if the number gets much larger than that, you'll start spreading yourself too thin (and you might even include someone who won't measure up to the job). So limit yourself to a *few* good men, not many.

These three guys should be men you can trust completely. Confidentiality is essential because you should feel free to talk with these guys about *anything and everything* (remember that confidentiality cuts both ways). And because these men are your most trusted advisors, they should also be fellow believers, strong Christians who don't mind exploring the Gospels as they hunker down with you in the foxholes of life. Simply put, you should choose three men who are always available, always loyal, always honest, always faithful, and always willing to help.

Because you're human, you will tend to become more and more like your closest counterparts—not *less* like them. So, your inner circle has the power to make you a *better* man (the kind of man God wants you to be) or a *lesser* man (the kind of guy society encourages you to be). And since your **3** will influence you in ways that are both subtle and powerful, you should select guys whom you really admire.

Can you, without too much hesitation, name at least three men who might fit smoothly into your inner circle? Do you trust these guys—and can they trust you—completely and without any hesitation? If so, you and your inner circle are blessed. And if not, it's time to start thinking very carefully about the nature, the quality, and the duration of your closest friendships.

WHEN THREE GUYS WENT INTO THE FIRE TOGETHER

If you'd like to know what can happen when three good men are willing to team up and take the heat *together*, you need look no further than the third chapter of Daniel. There, you'll find the story of three men who refused to kneel down and worship a statue of King Nebuchadnezzar even though just about everybody else in Babylon had decided to deify their crazy king.

For their trouble, this famous trio—Shadrach, Meshach, and Abednego—were sentenced (by Old Nebuchadnezzar himself) to a tortured death by fire, inside a blazing furnace, no less. But God had other plans. You see, when these courageous men were tied up and tossed into the flames, they were accompanied—and protected—by a mysterious "fourth man" who "looked like the Son of God."

Shadrach, Meshach, and Abednego weren't casual acquaintances who happened to bump into one another on the way to the execution chamber. No, they were close friends, ready to live together and, if necessary, to die together. They were like three strands woven together into a single rope, stronger together than they could ever be apart.

Can you imagine the conversations those men had in that fiery furnace? Wouldn't you like to have conversations like that with your closest friends? Well, you'll never experience those kinds of interactions *unless* you're willing to walk into—and through—the fire with them.

So the meaning of the story is clear: When three courageous men banded together for God, they were never alone. God entered the fire with them and shielded them from harm. And He'll do the same for your group *if* you let Him.

When you are in the furnace,
your Father keeps His eye on the clock
and His hand on the thermostat.
He knows just how much you can take.

Warren Wiersbe

FIVE THINGS TO LOOK FOR
WHEN SELECTING YOUR 3

Here are a few of the things you should expect from the men who comprise your inner circle:

1. **Total Honesty:** You should expect unvarnished honesty, without sugar-coating or spin. You just can't expect this kind of honest feedback from the people you bump into on the street, but you should expect it from your "**3**."

2. **Shared Values:** Select men whose values you admire and whose judgment you trust. These guys aren't perfect, but they'd like to be. And because they're constantly trying to improve themselves, their efforts are bound to rub off on you.

3. **Unwavering Loyalty:** In our no-deposit-no-return world, genuine loyalty is a vanishing commodity. The world may turn against you from time to time, but your inner circle must remain steadfast.

4. **Confidentiality:** Unless you're sure these guys can keep their mouths shut, you'll never be able to confide in them completely.

5. **Staying Power:** Although the men who comprise your group of **3** will probably change as you (or they) enter

different phases of life, this group shouldn't be a revolving door. In fact, it's possible that one or two guys will be your inner-circle confidants for life. It's more likely, of course, that you'll have several different inner circles as you grow older, and that's perfectly okay. But if you're trading in best buds faster than you trade cars, it's time to take stock of the way you make—and break—important relationships.

ACCOUNTABILITY IS ESSENTIAL

We live in a world where genuine accountability is the exception and "drive-by" accountability is the rule. Sure, we're willing to hold ourselves accountable when it's convenient, but we're quick to head for the exits when it's not. Yet there's an obvious problem with here-today-and-gone-tomorrow accountability: It inevitably leads to seat-of-the-pants decisions that can have dangerous consequences.

Every man is accountable to God, of course. Every man should also be accountable to a few close advisors, a few willing-to-get-in-his-face comrades who aren't afraid to offer friendly-but-frank communication (with a decided emphasis on "frank"). That's the kind of straightforward give-and-take that you should expect from your inner circle. It's a level of honesty that you can't expect from casual friends; it's above and beyond the ordinary.

In most relationships, people skim the surface—sure, they may be honest up to a point, but they're not *too* honest—so what you get is the truth with a little *t*. But with your group of **3** you should expect more; you should expect the unvarnished Truth, with a capital *T*. In fact, your three men should form a trio of truth—honest to a fault—because you need at least three guys on the planet who are willing to tell you what you *need* to hear, not what you *want* to hear. And make no mistake: You inhabit a world where honest, constructive criticism is still in very short supply.

Perhaps you're one of those guys who can't stand criticism, whether it's constructive or otherwise. Or maybe you're just a little too fond of trotting out that worn-out litany of excuses every time you feel a little heat. Or perhaps you're just the "sensitive" type, a fellow who can't stand the thought of confrontation. If so, get over it—you need honesty far more than you need to feed your own sensitivities.

Being accountable to your group of **3** means that you must forgo any excuse-making as you open up and tell your guys what's *actually* going on in your life: the sub-surface reality of your world, not the façade you may present to everybody else. If you don't open yourself up—or if you start shading the truth to your group of **3**—there's no way they can give you meaningful advice because they don't have all the facts.

Speaking of facts, do you remember the good old days when you, as a student, received six detailed evaluations a year? Those evaluations were called report cards, and you probably dreaded them like a chicken dreads a fox convention. Well, things have changed plenty since then. Now that you're a fully-grown man, the days of regular monthly report cards are forever gone. Today, you're probably lucky to receive one or two evaluations a year, usually at work, and oftentimes they contain more fluff than substance. So what's a man to do? Well, for starters, you can—and should—depend upon your closest friends to give you honest, excuse-free feedback about your performance as a Christian, as a family man, and as a working man.

But why do you need help evaluating the man in the mirror? After all, shouldn't you be able to grade yourself? Well, not exactly. You're simply too close to that guy in the mirror to be objective, and you're only able to see yourself from one angle. So sometimes, you'll be tempted to give yourself straight A's when you deserve considerably lower grades. Or, you may become your own worst critic, giving yourself a string of failing marks when you deserve better. The truth, of course, is often somewhere in the middle. And your inner circle can give you the honest feedback you need to view yourself as realistically as possible.

Spiritual growth is the process
of replacing falsehood with truth.

Rick Warren

GOOD DECISIONS ARE MADE IN ADVANCE, NOT BY IMPULSE

Most of us guys are at least a little bit impulsive, so we're tempted to make big decisions without taking time to fully consider the downside risks. We tend to act first and think second (sometimes, it seems, engaging the brain only as a last resort). And when we do, we can get ourselves into big trouble.

If you've ever been victimized by your own impulsive decision-making—or by the impulsive decisions of others— you understand how important it is to look carefully before you leap. But sometimes, one set of eyeballs just isn't enough. That's why you need an "accountability group" (composed of your inner circle of **3**) to help you look things over before the time for leaping arrives.

So here's the one-two-three punch that KOs dumb decisions:

1. Train yourself to pray about everything, even if your prayers are quick, open-eyed conversations with your Heavenly Father.

2. Rely upon a clear set of principles (before) and take action (after). And while you're deciding what principles to live by, be sure that everything you stand for can be backed up by specific references from God's Word (and

while you're reading, be sure to pay close attention to the book of Proverbs; it's filled with important insights).

3. And if you're about to make a big decision, be sure to talk things over with your **3** guys *before* you make a final decision, not *after*.

When you take these three steps, you'll make solid decisions (not impulsive ones), and you'll avoid needless headaches and heartbreaks.

CLOSE FRIENDS SHOULD BE WILLING TO CONFRONT EACH OTHER

Sometimes a true friend needs to step into your life and confront you face-to-face. When it happens, you should be big enough (and smart enough) to let him into your world and into your thoughts. Why? Because a true friend can sometimes save you from danger, even disgrace, if you let him deal with you nose-to-nose.

It takes a strong man to give someone else access to his life. Are you that kind of man? Can you listen to personal criticism without taking offense, or are you one of those thin-skinned guys who can't stand to hear anything but praise? If you're willing to listen to constructive criticism with an open mind, you'll be doing yourself a big, big favor. But if you're a hardheaded fellow who can't bear criticism, even when it's deserved, you're depriving yourself of valuable information, information that you may desperately need. In order to get that information, you need to disclose "the whole truth" to your closest friends.

As the old saying goes, "Sometimes the greatest un-truths are told in silence." In other words, withholding the truth can be, at times, just as harmful as telling a lie. As you think about your communications with your **3**, remember this: You should be confident enough to be candid, and you should expect your friends to be equally candid with you.

While it's probably not a good idea to surround yourself with a chorus of full-time critics, you should be willing to listen to the honest appraisals of your closest friends, even when their evaluations are negative. So when a close friend tells you that you're heading down a dead-end street, it's time to think long and hard about turning yourself around before you run headlong into trouble.

The Whole Truth

You should be confident enough with your **3** to tell "the whole truth and nothing but the truth": If you're ever tempted to withhold the truth from a member of your inner circle, slow down for a minute and ask yourself what you're afraid of, or what you're hiding from.

EVEN JESUS DEPENDED ON
A FEW GOOD MEN

Christ had a dozen disciples, but He was closer to some than others. In the Gospels, we learn that Jesus confided more to—and seems to have had a special relationship with—three disciples: James, John, and Simon Peter.

James is believed by many scholars to be Jesus' first cousin. Because he was bold and energetic, James was called a "son of thunder." And he was a dynamic disciple and the first apostle to be glorified through martyrdom.

John (also called a "son of thunder") was certainly part of Christ's innermost circle (Matthew 17:1, 26:37). And after Christ's betrayal, it was John and Simon Peter who followed Christ when others retreated (in fact, it was Jesus Himself who changed Simon's name to Peter, which meant, literally, "a mass of the rock." Jesus knew that Peter would be the rock upon which His earthly church would be built).

Shortly before His crucifixion, Jesus went into the garden at Gethsemane to pray. And whom did He take with Him? Not surprisingly, it was His three most trusted advisors: James, John, and Peter. And it was to John and Peter that Mary first brought the glorious news of Christ's resurrection. So it's no surprise that John and Peter were the first two disciples to go and see the risen Christ.

Yes, even Jesus had an inner circle, a few good men in whom He could confide. And if it worked for Him, it can work for you, too.

KEEPING THINGS IN PERSPECTIVE

Your group of **3** will help you keep things in perspective. And here in the modern world, you're likely to need at least four brains (theirs and yours) to navigate the challenges of everyday life.

For most men, life is busy and complicated. Amid the rush and crush of the daily grind, it is easy to lose focus. When your world seems to be spinning out of control, you must seek to regain perspective by slowing yourself down, by talking to your closest confidants, and by turning your thoughts toward God.

The familiar words of Psalm 46:10 remind us to "Be still, and know that I am God" (NKJV). And the words of Proverbs 27:17 make clear that "As iron sharpens iron, a friend sharpens a friend" (NLT). Yes, a solid inner circle can help you sharpen your skills and focus your thoughts.

So do yourself a favor: today and every day, be open to God's instruction and be open to your friends' advice. When you do, you can face the day's complications with wisdom, with perspective, with strength, and with hope.

If a temporary loss of perspective has left you worried, exhausted, or both, it's time to readjust your thought patterns. Negative thoughts are habit-forming; thankfully, so are positive ones. With practice—and with a little help from your closest comrades—you can form the habit of focusing on God's priorities and your own possibilities. When you do, you'll soon discover that you will spend less time worrying about your challenges and more time solving them.

Have you ever gazed out over a string of molehills and imagined that you were looking at the Himalayas? If so, you're not alone. Everybody loses perspective from time to time. But if you make a *habit* of turning molehills into mountains, you'll discover that those imaginary peaks will soon become volcanic. So, if you've been wasting time and energy fretting about the consequences of some distant possibility, think again. After all, no one ever changed the future by dreading it. So, instead of worrying about tomorrow, do today's work and leave the rest up to God. When you do, you'll discover that if you do your part today, the future has a way of taking care of itself.

God is bigger than your problems.
Whatever worries press upon you today,
put them in God's hands and leave them there.

Billy Graham

THINGS TO LOOK FOR AS YOUR INNER CIRCLE CHANGES OVER TIME

Your Age	Things to Consider as You Choose Your Inner Circle
Approximately Ages 20 to 30	In early adulthood, you're figuring out what it means to be a *real* man as you face up to *real* responsibilities. So look for fellow believers whose values you trust. And while you're at it, look for at least one older man who can give you solid, big-picture advice about your marriage, your career, your future, and your faith.
Approximately Ages 30 to 50	These are years when it's easy to fall for the hollow promises that the world makes but cannot deliver. So look for men who keep you focused on God's values, not the world's values. Find friends who can help you keep your head on straight during these demanding—and at times dangerous—years.
Approximately Ages 50 to 65	For many, these are the most productive years both professionally and personally. As a result, some guys become overly impressed with their own accomplishments. If you're a midlife male who's hitting your stride, find friends who can keep you humble, centered, involved, and (it's worth repeating), humble.
Approximately Ages 65 and Beyond	As the reality of eternity becomes more clearly etched in your brain, look for friends who help you finish strong by staying involved in your faith and your discipleship. You may also look for a few good younger men who need *you* to be *their* mentor.

A FEW MAN-TO-MAN QUESTIONS FOR YOU

1. Do you have at least three inner-circle friends with whom you can be completely honest? And if not, what are you going to do about it? In the space below, name your inner-circle friends:

_____

_____

_____

_____

2. Are you trustworthy? Prove it by going to three close friends and ask them if they'd share something in confidence with you. Then, record your results by selecting the sentence (A, B, or C) that best describes the answers you receive:

   A. All three friends indicate that you're completely trustworthy. That means they'd tell you just about anything. These responses show that you're a reliable, mature, non-gossipy guy. Congratulations.

   B. At least one of your friends indicates that he might be somewhat hesitant to share a big secret with you. This response means that you probably still have a thing or two to learn about confidentiality.

C. Two or three of the guys you talk to express reservations about sharing confidential info with you. This means you've still got some growing up to do. And the best day to begin growing up is this one.

3. Pick the sentence below (A, B, or C) that best describes you:

A. You're willing to listen to—and learn from—closest friends when they hold you accountable for your actions.

B. When your closest friends call you to account, you may not like what you hear—and you may not take their advice—but you're not hostile.

C. You simply cannot stand the idea of other people "telling you what to do," so you don't welcome—and you do not usually accept—advice from anybody, even your closest friends.

WHAT NEXT?

Okay, now that you've seen the need for a three-man inner circle, what are you going to do about it? Here are several things you can and should do:

1. If you're not yet the kind of man whom your closest friends can trust completely, it's time to grow up. Remember that your inner circle of **3** will never be effective until you find the courage and the wisdom to be totally trustworthy.

2. Talk to God about the three guys who should make up your inner circle. If you're not certain who your **3** guys are, take the next three weeks and pray about your decision. And if God only reveals one of two men to you, start there and wait for God to help you fill out your small group at a time of His choosing.

3. Once you've settled on the names of the men who comprise your small group, write their names in the space below. Pray for them and approach them individually to discuss their being a part of your inner circle. Make sure that your discussions are face-to-face, not over the phone.

_____

_____

_____

12

1   3   **12**   120   3000

FORTIFY YOURSELF WITH A FLOCK OF
FRIENDS! YOU CAN WRITE TO ONE,
DINE WITH ONE, VISIT ONE, OR TAKE
YOUR PROBLEMS TO ONE. THERE IS
ALWAYS AT LEAST ONE WHO WILL
UNDERSTAND, INSPIRE, AND GIVE YOU
THE LIFT YOU MAY NEED AT THE TIME.

—

George Matthew Adams

The third number in The ManCode is **12**, a number that signifies a broader circle of good friends—men you can do things with, men you can share good times with, men who can help you get things done. Of course Jesus enlisted a dozen disciples who came from varied backgrounds. And you need at least a dozen men who, while certainly not as close as your inner circle of 3, comprise your own personal network of go-to guys.

The first two numbers in The ManCode are straight-forward: the number 1 signifies your relationship with God, and it's non-negotiable. The number 3 signifies a clearly identified "accountability team" composed of Christian men who will help you plan for the future and who will hold you accountable for your actions. But your group of **12** may not be quite so easy to identify because these men may have differing perspectives and differing backgrounds.

Will some of the men in your **12** be from your church? Probably so, but not all of them should be. You probably need more variety than that.

Will all the members of your **12** ever gather in one place? Probably not. In fact, unless you're living in a very small town, some of the men in your **12** may not even know one another.

Should all the men in this expanded circle be Chris-tians? Probably not, and that's good because it gives you the opportunity to reach out and share your faith with good friends. But what is certain is this: Each man in your **12** should make a positive contribution to your life. That means that each man in your **12** should be a source of *positive* peer pressure—a constructive influence in a decidedly negative world.

As you think about the guys who will comprise this larger circle of friends, look for men who:

1. You enjoy being with;

2. Are available;

3. Are boosters, not cynics;

4. Exert a positive influence on your life.

So don't be concerned if you can easily name more than a dozen guys who might fit into your **12**. But on the other hand, if you've wracked your brain and you still can't name twelve good men, it's time to start expanding your reach.

AT LEAST ONE MEMBER OF YOUR 3 MAY ALSO BE IN YOUR *12*

Can you have crossover friends who do double duty in both your 3 and your **12**? Of course you can. But it's probably a good idea to have at least one member of your inner 3 who is clearly *outside* the social landscape of your **12**. Why?

Because you need at least one key advisor who can help you engage in outside-the-box thinking, and that probably means that you need at least one man who isn't completely immersed in the everyday realities of your world.

Your 3 won't change much over time, but this is not so for your **12**. While you shouldn't consider your **12** to be a revolving-door group of quick-changing acquaintances, neither should you expect the group to be permanent. After all, because you're dealing with the lives and careers of *at least* a dozen men, you should expect—and even welcome— a certain amount of change within the group.

And by the way, if you're heavily involved in your community, you may have several groups of **12**. You might, for example, be a member of a tight-knit men's Bible study group *and* an active participant in a local service club *and* a booster at your kid's school *and* a contributing member of the local business community, *and* the list goes on.

CAN A NON-CHRISTIAN
BE IN YOUR GROUP OF *12*?

It's ironic that some guys, especially those who take their faith seriously, seem hesitant to establish meaningful friendships with non-Christians. The irony, of course, stems from the fact that Christ Himself created a ministry that reached out to *everybody*; Jesus didn't isolate Himself in the relative safety of a few likeminded believers. Far from it. Christ extended Himself to Jews and Gentiles, to rich and poor, to sinners and to saints. And if it was good enough for Him, it's good enough for you.

One of the great experiences for a Christian man is to lead another man to Christ. But guess what? If you never have a meaningful conversation with a non-believer, you're unlikely to lead *anybody* to Jesus.

So don't hesitate to establish friendships outside the church. You are the light, and you're only here on earth for a short visit. While you're here, you should shine as brightly—and as widely—as you can.

MEN NEED TO SPEND TIME WITH OTHER MEN

Whoever said, "It's a man's world," wasn't living in the twenty-first century. Today, the differences between the sexes are seldom celebrated and often minimized. Whether it's in the workplace or at the local health club, or just about anyplace in between, men and women are tossed in together, usually with far too little time for guy-to-guy interaction.

In the good old days, if you went to the local YMCA to work out, you entered an all-guy world, a place where you could really be yourself. But today, if you're down at the Y sweating off a few pounds on the treadmill, you may be surrounded by women, with scarcely another man in sight. It's no longer a man's world—for better or worse, it's a coed world, pure and simple. But just because the world doesn't see the value of guys hanging out with guys doesn't mean that you should go along with the idea. You need good men—and more than a few of them—to hang out with, to talk with, to learn from, to have fun with, and to accomplish things with.

And while you're with your **12**, you shouldn't constantly feel compelled to give sermons, to lecture, to preach, or to teach theology. The best way to show another guy that you're a Christian is to behave like one. When you do the simple things—like counting every single stroke on the golf course or refusing to take a second look at a woman in a short skirt who passes by—you may disclose more about your faith than if you had delivered a year's worth of sermons. So think of your **12** not as a flock that needs to be preached to, but as a group of guys who can help you enjoy the game of life while you're improving your skills. Even if you're very good at what you do, your skills can still be sharpened. And your **12** can help.

God has a plan for your friendships because
He knows your friends determine
the quality and direction of your life.

Charles Stanley

BETRAYAL IS A POSSIBILITY

Jesus chose Judas in His **12**, knowing that in the fullness of time, Judas would betray Him. And even Peter, in a moment of weakness, denied Christ.

You, like the Master, may experience betrayal within your group of **12**. So don't expect that every man in the group will be perfectly loyal or trustworthy. In fact, please don't be surprised if you're sold out by a member of this group. But if you're betrayed, remember that the disloyalty, as painful as it may be, is still part of God's plan for your life. Could it be that the lesson in the betrayal is more important than the fun and the friendship? Probably so.

Sometimes, you must accept the fact that occasional betrayals are simply part of God's grand design—and that grace is always available to the betrayer. After all, Peter became the rock of the church *after* he betrayed Christ.

God has a plan for the life of every Christian.
Every circumstance, every turn of destiny,
all things work together for your good and for His glory.

Billy Graham

A FEW MAN-TO-MAN QUESTIONS FOR YOU

1. Can you name about a dozen men who can form a strong circle of friends—men you can spend time with, have fun with, and learn from? If so, list those men below.

_____

_____

_____

_____

_____

_____

_____

_____

_____

_____

_____

_____

_____

_____

_____

_____

_____

_____

2. Now that you've listed at least a dozen men, list each guy again and give him a grade on a sliding scale from 1 to 10, with 10 meaning that he has a totally positive impact on your life and 1 meaning that he has become a real negative influence. After you've graded each man on your list, consider carefully what the list says about the nature, the quality, and the future direction of your friendships. And while you're at it, please don't be impatient with the imperfections of your friends, just as you hope they won't be impatient with yours.

_____	_____
_____	_____
_____	_____
_____	_____
_____	_____
_____	_____
_____	_____
_____	_____
_____	_____
_____	_____
_____	_____
_____	_____
_____	_____

As you think about the men you've described on the previous page, remember that God cares for every person on that list, and so should you. So don't ostracize a friend just because you've given him a low rating. Instead of giving up on him, try a different approach . . . try leading him to Christ.

3. Rate yourself as a **12**. If all your friends were like you, would your friendships be stronger, weaker, or non-existent?

_____

_____

_____

_____

_____

_____

_____

_____

_____

_____

_____

_____

_____

120

1   3   12   **120**   3000

THE BIBLE KNOWS NOTHING OF SOLITARY RELIGION.

—

John Wesley

The next number in The ManCode is **120**—a number that stands for the local church. In the second chapter of Acts, we are told that shortly after Christ ascended into heaven, **120** of His disciples were touched by the Holy Spirit. This small but powerful group of men became the foundation of the early church, so we've chosen the number **120** to represent Christ's church. And make no mistake: you and I *are* the church. When we come into a relationship with Jesus, we, like believers of every generation, become like Peter, of whom Christ said, "Upon this rock I will build my church" (vv. Matthew 16:18 KJV). So please don't think of the church as merely a free-standing collection of bricks and mortar because it's more than that. Much more!

Far too many folks go to church for the wrong reasons: to get something from other members or to put an imaginary checkmark on some self-imposed cosmic to-do list or to fulfill some family tradition or simply out of habit. But none of these reasons is good enough. Why, then, should you get yourself out of bed (or off the golf course) to worship God in His church? It's simple:

You should go to church to grow and to give.

If your church allows you to continue growing in your faith—and if you've found a place where you can enthusiastically give of your talents, your treasure, and your time—you're worshipping at the right place. But if you're simply taking up space on a pew for an hour or two on Sunday mornings—and if you're not totally sure why you're sitting there—it's time to rethink your priorities, your place of worship, and your participation. And while you're thinking, remember that if you have a problem with the church, the problem probably has as much (or more) to do with *you* than with the church you're attending.

You won't *get* much out of any church unless you're willing to *give* something to that church (and the "something" we're talking about here is not necessarily money). If you ever stop giving to the church, you'll soon become disgruntled. So the only way you'll *really* be satisfied in a church is to be a contributing member of your church—there's really no other way. And what happens if you become burned out on church? The answer is to become *more* involved, not *less*.

And please don't get too hung up on the physical structure where worship takes place. Can church happen in a basement in China? Of course it can. And does it happen at the biggest mega-church on the planet? Certainly. And can it happen anyplace in between? Absolutely. God says, "Where two or three are gathered together in My name, I am there among them" (Matthew 18:20 Holman CSB). So the size of your church or its physical characteristics aren't nearly as important as the size of the things you experience there.

Church is a place to fill yourself up and to give yourself away. It's a place where you become a part of something much bigger than yourself. It's a place where 2 + 2 may equal 5, or

5,000, or 5,000,000. This kind of supernatural multiplication occurs *through* the church because God chooses to bless the efforts *of* His church. Whether it's a missions trip to a foreign land, disaster relief after a hurricane, or using five loaves and two fish to feed thousands, God always partners with His church to bless their efforts.

GIVE YOUR KIDS THAT OLD-TIME RELIGION

Not so long ago, before the advent of the modern media—back in the days when typical youngsters still performed manual labor and lots of it—young folks flocked to church because it was one of the few places where they could be with other kids. After working six hard days (often in the fields), youngsters viewed church as a welcome change of pace. So they didn't dread church; they embraced it.

Yes, in the good old days, the church was not only the center of family life, but also the center of community life. Not so anymore. In today's world, "popular culture" seems to have taken the place of the church as the foundation of societal values, and we're worse off because of it. So it's no wonder that our young people are struggling to find their way in a world that honors materialism and instant gratification, not morality.

Common sense tells us—and the Bible teaches us—that it's important to introduce our youngsters to the church at an early age. So if you're a dedicated dad who wants what's best for your kids (and if you're a dedicated dad, you do), you'll make certain that your youngsters are in church and that you're right there with them.

So here are some timely questions: What are you going to do to make church as attractive to your children as it was to your grandparents when they were kids? Are you going to give up or give more . . . more to your family, more to the church, and more to God?

YOU NEED THE CHURCH MORE THAN THE CHURCH NEEDS YOU

Perhaps you've been under the misconception that the church needs you. Well, not exactly. You see, you need the church *far more* than the church needs you. This certainly doesn't mean that the church won't benefit from your help, and it doesn't mean that you shouldn't be a contributing member to your local fellowship. But what it does mean is this: If you're doing things right, you'll *always* get more out of a church than you put into it.

God doesn't need for you to attend church; *you* need the experience of attending, as Hebrews 10:24-25 explains, "Let's see how inventive we can be in encouraging love and helping out, not avoiding worshipping together as some do but spurring each other on" (MSG). God doesn't need your money; *you* need the experience of giving it to Him. God doesn't need your time or your talents—He already has infinite quantities of those—but *you* need the experience of sharing. God clearly can accomplish His work without your assistance, but He desires to work through you so that you can be blessed in the process.

You need the fellowship and the gifts you can find in the local church. You need the variety of people you find there: people with different personalities, professions, and attitudes; people who will be there for you and your family when you need them. Without the church, you are like a single burning coal that's separated from the fire; you'll lose energy and heat. And you don't want that to happen. That's why fellowship with other believers should be an integral part of your everyday life.

You also need to witness the supernatural multiplication that can happen when a church *really* gets serious about changing the world. You need to see firsthand the marvelous things that God can do when cooperative Christians reach out to the needy. You need to be an eyewitness—and an active participant—in the mission field. You need to see how congregations can transform the lives of people around the corner or around the globe. And you need to witness these things as part of a team, not as a soloist.

Jesus understood networking. When He wanted to share His message, He called upon His church to help do it. And nothing has changed since then. Today, God wants the world to see His church in action. That's why Christians are often the first (and most effective) responders to natural disasters (think Katrina). And it's why so many churches help form the backbone of organizations like Habitat for Humanity.

Whether your church has **120** souls, 1,200, or 12,000, it is meant to be a powerful tool for spreading God's Good News and uplifting His people. God intends for you to be a fully contributing member of the church. And if you know what's good for you, your intentions will be the same.

About Going to Church

The church is not an end in itself; it is a means to the end of the kingdom of God.

E. Stanley Jones

The church is where it's at. The first place of Christian service for any Christian is in a local church.

Jerry Clower

Only participation in the full life of a local church builds spiritual muscle.

Rick Warren

MEN WITH BACKBONE SHOULD BE
THE BACKBONE OF THE CHURCH

If you visit any church, it's easy to gauge the health of that church by looking at the folks who are sitting in the pews. If there are plenty of fully-grown, church-loving, Bible-believing, fellowship-building men who are present and accounted for, the church is in good shape. But if you see many more women than men, you should ask yourself, "Where have all the guys gone? Are they all down at the bowling alley or at the lake fishing or on the golf course or out at the softball diamond? And why have they abandoned their church?"

That isn't to say, of course, that God doesn't call women to contribute mightily to His church—of course He does. But in far too many congregations, it seems that women are being asked to do most of the heavy lifting. Why? Because when it comes to the vital business of building the local church, far too many men are missing in action.

Men need to be actively involved in the church because we were made for the church—it's our natural home. That's why we should *never* sit back and let the women do most of the work and most of the worship. Instead, we must stand up and be counted. We need to see more fathers worshipping with children, more husbands worshipping with wives, and more men taking leadership roles in the church. We need men to provide strength and stability in the church. We need more men's classes, more men's groups, and more men's ministries . . . yes, we need them badly and we need them *now*.

It's true that many churches don't seem to be "man-friendly"—it's almost as if they were catering to a feminine demographic. And while much more could be written on this subject, suffice it to say that the local church is ministering to the people who are coming through their doors, and most of those folks, at least in recent years, happen to be women. This trend, by the way, is quite a change from the days of old.

In Old Testament times, women weren't even *allowed* inside certain parts of the Temple. But we're living in New Testament times, which means we worship together—men side-by-side with women—and thank goodness we do. Yet too many fully-grown guys are missing that opportunity, the opportunity of worshipping alongside their wives and children. Make sure you're not one of them.

UNCLE SAM ISN'T THE ONLY ONE WHO NEEDS YOU

Every American is familiar with Uncle Sam, the star-spangled personification of our nation's patriotism. In fact, if you close your eyes right now, you can probably see Sam, clad in red, white, and blue, pointing his finger squarely (and seriously) in your direction as he says, "I want you!"

Well, Uncle Sam isn't the only man who needs your help; your pastor needs it, too. Why? Because your pastor is doing the most important work of all: the work of sharing the message of God's Son. Of course all the numbers of The ManCode are directly related to Jesus, our Shepherd. But the number 120 addresses the special relationship that you should have with God's "under-shepherd": your pastor.

Jesus Himself was surrounded and supported by men. We men, in turn, must surround and support our pastors because they're our leaders, the shepherds who protect our own particular flocks. We must honor each pastor's calling and recognize his role in God's kingdom. Being a pastor is a demanding, seven-day-a-week job, a job with more pressures than most of us realize. And sometimes, pastoring a church can be a lonely endeavor. So you can be sure that your minister, like Uncle Sam, needs as many good men as he can muster.

Your pastor needs men to help build the church and serve its members. He needs honest, clear-thinking friends to advise him, and he needs trustworthy men to watch his back when times get tough. Your pastor even needs men to help him find other men, new members who, in turn, can help grow the church by pitching in and rolling up their sleeves for the Lord. In short, your pastor needs men like you, men who are ready, willing, and able to serve.

Your pastor is worthy of his hire; he answers to the Lord; and he must someday give an accounting of his work. A man with such demands and responsibilities needs genuine counsel, courtesy, compassion and encouragement. He needs more than a few good men—in fact, he needs a church full of them—men who, by working together, can become an army of One.

Perhaps you can be an inner-circle 3 to your pastor. Or maybe you will become a member of his 12. But in any event, you should always strive to be a contributing member of his 120. No exceptions!

So if you take no other idea from this book, please remember these three words: "Support your pastor." He deserves your help, and you deserve the experience of giving it to him.

TEN (MYTHICAL) REASONS NOT TO GO TO CHURCH WITH (REAL) RESPONSES IN PARENTHESIS

Reason # 1: Everybody in church is a hypocrite.
(No, *everybody* in church *isn't* a hypocrite, and your own negativity doesn't make it a reality.)

Reason #2: The church doesn't meet my needs.
(Lots of people in the church are trying *hard* to meet your needs. Are you looking *past* these folks or *for* them?)

Reason #3: Church takes up too much time.
(Sure church takes time. But so does watching the Golf Channel, the NFL, NASCAR, and *American Idol*. And which is more important?)

Reason #4: They're always asking for money. (No, they're not *always* asking for money. And besides, if every guy gave what he *should* give, the church wouldn't need to ask for money.)

Reason #5: I don't like the preacher.
(The preacher is trying to get through to you. How hard are you trying to *let him* get through?)

Reason #6: I had a bad experience in the church.
(No place is perfect. You've had bad experiences everywhere: at work, at home, at school, and just about every place in between. But you probably didn't quit work or drop out of school at the first sign of trouble, and if you did give up, the common denominator is you.)

Reason #7: The music is too loud.
(Really?)

Reason #8: The music isn't loud enough.
(If so, why are you still sitting in the last pew?)

Reason #9: The Sunday School classes are boring.
(Your church obviously needs a few more good teachers. By the way, when was the last time you taught?)

Reason #10: Someone sat in my pew last week. (Your pew? Maybe the trespasser thought it was God's pew.)

A FEW MAN-TO-MAN QUESTIONS FOR YOU

1. Besides giving money, can you list at least three other ways you've contributed to the life of your church during the last six months. Write them on the lines below.

_____

_____

_____

_____

_____

_____

_____

_____

2. If everybody else in your church contributed as much as you do, would your church be stronger, weaker, about the same—or out of business?

_____

_____

_____

_____

3. How creative can you be in thinking of ways to contribute to the life of your church? On the lines below, list at least five new ideas for service—five things you can do during the coming year to strengthen your church.

_____

_____

_____

_____

_____

_____

_____

_____

_____

_____

_____

_____

_____

_____

_____

WHAT NEXT?

1. If you're not involved in a local church, the most important thing on your to-do list is to find one that fits you and your family. On the lines below jot down some of the things you would like in a church. And, spend time in prayer over the next several days asking God to direct you. Now, be proactive, start this Sunday visiting churches in your area.

_____

_____

_____

_____

_____

_____

2. Can you point to three ways you've grown as a result of attending church?

_____

_____

_____

_____

_____

_____

3. If you're already a member of a church, take an inventory of your participation on the lines below. Are you really active, or are you just taking up space? Be brutally honest with yourself, and make note of specific things you can do to *give* more to your church and to *grow* more in your faith.

_____

_____

_____

_____

_____

_____

_____

_____

_____

_____

_____

_____

_____

_____

_____

_____

3000

1   3   12   120   3000

JESUS CALLS US
NOT ONLY TO COME TO HIM,
BUT TO GO FOR HIM.

—

Rick Warren

The ManCode ends back where it began: by taking a careful look at your relationship with God. The first number of The ManCode deals directly with your One-to-one relationship with the Creator. And the final number in The ManCode, the number **3000**, deals directly with your response to God's calling—a mission that He has placed deep in your heart—your calling to serve others.

Think for a moment about the early Christian church in the days immediately after Christ's ascension into heaven: the 11 disciples along with Matthias (the man who replaced Judas so that the disciples might once again form a complete group of 12) gathered with 120 new Christians, all crowded into the Upper Room, that sacred place where the last supper had been served less than two months before. Many of these men had just spent 40 days with the risen Christ, but now Jesus was gone.

On that same day that the 120 gathered in the Upper Room, Peter spoke to a large group in Jerusalem, and **3000** men and women were baptized. This occurred on the day that was the Jewish feast of Pentecost, a day that was a defining moment in the early church.

So the number **3000** stands for *reach* and *service*—your need to reach out to the world by translating God's Good News into your own good deeds.

Jesus had clear instructions for all His disciples: "Go into all the world and preach the gospel to the whole creation" (Mark 16:15 Holman CSB). But Jesus wasn't implying that all of us should become preachers—He knew from experience that most guys wouldn't stand up in front of a crowd and give a sermon. No, Jesus wanted us to preach His gospel, not just with our mouths but with our hands and feet. And that's what the number **3000** is about: It's about serving God by going out into the world and serving others.

THE TUG

Have you ever felt God tugging on your heart? Have you ever had the feeling that God wanted you to go somewhere or do something for Him? Have you ever felt the need to give more, to sacrifice more, or to do more for God by doing more for His children—whether those people were located on the other side of town or on the other side of the globe? The honest answer to each of these questions (whether you realize it or not) is yes.

Every day of your life, God is tugging you in a particular direction, the direction He wants you to go. But if you're like most of us hardheaded men, you may be resisting that tug. After all, you already have your own strategy and your own to-do list (not to mention your own wish list). And if you're like most males, you secretly want to be a take-charge kind of guy, a rugged individualist who charts his own course, picks his own fights, solves his own problems, feeds his own appetites, and makes his own plans. But the trouble begins when *your* plans don't bear any resemblance to *God's* plans—and when that happens, something's got to give.

Some men spend entire lifetimes resisting God's tug. Like lounge singers doing a poor Sinatra imitation, they insist upon doing things *My Way* instead of *His* way. And by resisting God's call, they miss out on the best that life has to offer.

Other men—and we sincerely hope you'll include yourself in their number—finally respond to God's tug. They realize that the tug they feel comes from the Creator of the universe, and they respond accordingly. They ask God for guidance, they listen for His responses, they step beyond their comfort zones, and they begin doing big things *for Him*. These men are the real heroes of God's kingdom. These are the men who lead the families, who build the churches, who serve the local communities, and who reach out to the world. These are the dads, the coaches, the boosters, the mentors, the Big Brothers, the chaplains, the Sunday School teachers, and the Scout masters who help make the world better one kid at a time. These are the guys who are willing to get involved—and stay involved—in the life of their church, in the lives of their friends, and in the lives of people they don't even know. These are the men who are *really* responding to Christ's great commission. They're taking the gospel out into the world, and they're preaching it—sometimes with words but more often with work. They're doing things *with* God and *for* God. And when they do, they've successfully dialed in The ManCode's final number.

God's tug is not a push—He will not force you to do something against your will. But what He will do is this: He will stand at the door of your heart and invite you to help others. He will lead you to people who need your help, and He will invite you to help them. He certainly won't compel you to help; He'll encourage you to help. The rest is up to you.

And how can you be absolutely certain that the tugs you feel are from God? Simple: God's tug always leads you to do something for others, not for yourself. The tug, if it is from God, is not about getting more things for you; it's never about more money, more possessions, more fame, more pleasure, or more gratification. No, God's tug isn't about getting; it's about giving—giving more of yourself to others.

But there's a paradox: by giving things away, you always receive more in return than you gave; it's simply another form of spiritual multiplication. That's why the Bible says, "It is more blessed to give than to receive" (Acts 20:35 NKJV).

When you answer God's tug, you've formed a partnership with the Creator of the universe. And the time to form that partnership is now.

DISCIPLESHIP NOW

Jesus' disciples came from all walks of life: blue collar and professionals, including fishermen and a tax collector. They were from different political spectrums, including some passionate zealots. These men came with diverse personalities and emotional traits, from Peter the impulsive to Thomas the doubter.

God is still in the business of acquiring disciples: ditch diggers and presidents; Republicans, Democrats, and Independents; introverts and extroverts. His only criterion is that you *believe* in Him and that you be willing to *live* for Him.

God has blessed you with unique opportunities to serve, and He has given you every tool that you need to do so. Today, accept this challenge: Value the talent that God has given you, nourish it, make it grow, and share it with the world. After all, the best way to say "Thank You" for God's gifts is to use them.

God wants you to "stay sharp" in His work . . . and you can do so by using The ManCode as your guide. So keep God as your Number-One priority, stay close to your friends, and be an active participant in your church, and keep reaching out to the world. And remember that The ManCode is an ongoing work. It's like when you go to the gym: You must unlock your locker every day. Unlocking your potential is an everyday activity . . . and your combination is:

1   3   12   120   3000.

HOW TO SHARE THE MANCODE

In his second letter to Timothy, Paul speaks to believers of every generation when he writes, "God has not given us a spirit of timidity" (1:7 NASB). Paul's meaning is clear: When sharing our testimonies, we must be courageous, forthright, and unashamed.

When we let other people know the details of our faith, we assume an important responsibility: the responsibility of making certain that our words are reinforced by our actions. When we share our testimonies, we must also be willing to serve as positive role models—undeniable examples of the changes that Jesus makes in the lives of those who accept Him as their personal Savior.

So here's a word of caution: Don't share The ManCode with others unless you're willing to live The ManCode. Why? Because the things you say about your faith are not nearly as important as the way you live your faith.

Genuine faith, the kind of faith that moves hearts and mountains, is better demonstrated than announced. In other words, it's perfectly fine to tell people about your beliefs, but it's far more effective to show them the results of your beliefs. And the good news is this: When you live your faith—day in and day out, in good times and hard times—other men do notice. After all, most of us guys are more interested in results than theories. We may listen to the things other people say, but we watch even more carefully what other people do.

We are, by and large, like the good folks from Missouri, the "Show Me State." We like things we can see "up close and personal." Then, we make judgments for ourselves.

When we can see with our own two eyes that The Man-Code is working for another guy, we're more likely to buy into the program. If not, we're likely to walk away sooner rather than later. So if you make The ManCode your personal code, remember that's it's never enough to talk about The ManCode; you also should make up your mind to become a living, breathing example of The ManCode in action.

About Discipleship

Our Lord is searching for people who will make
a difference. Christians dare not dissolve
into the background or blend into
the neutral scenery of the world.

Charles Swindoll

If it doesn't affect your hands and feet,
it isn't Christianity.

Jess Moody

A FEW MAN-TO-MAN QUESTIONS FOR YOU

1. Now that you're up to speed on all of The ManCode numbers, do you honestly believe that this Code can work for you?

   Answer yes or no: _____

2. If you answered no to question #1, what sort of personal code are you living by today, and what code do you intend to live by tomorrow?

   _____

   _____

   _____

3. If you answered yes to #1. above, give yourself a letter grade (A, B, C, D, or F) that represents your own assessment of how you're currently addressing each number in The ManCode:

   Your Relationship to 1:   Grade: ____
   Your 3:   Grade: ____
   Your 12:   Grade: ____
   Your 120:   Grade: ____
   Your 3000   Grade: ____

By the way, if you just gave yourself straight A's, perhaps it's time for some honest self-evaluation (unless, of course, you're a modern-day saint which, by the way, you probably aren't).

But what if your grades were less than spectacular? If so, don't beat yourself up. Just focus on the areas that need improvement, and start doing whatever it takes to improve your grades.

WHAT NEXT?

Now that you've graded yourself, it's time to let a few other folks grade you, too. Ask three or four people—and if you're married, ask your wife—to give you a letter grade (A, B, C, D, or F) for each number in The ManCode. Ask each person to offer candid assessments—be sure to discourage flattery and encourage honesty. Then, jot down their evaluations in the spaces below.

	1	3	12	120	3000
1. _____					
2. _____					
3. _____					
4. _____					

Were you surprised by anybody's assessment? What do your friends' and family's grades, combined with your own, have to say about the condition of your spiritual health? And what areas of The ManCode need immediate attention?

AND FINALLY: IT'S YOUR CHOICE

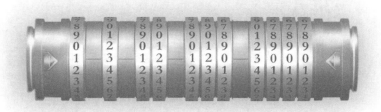

1   3   12   120   3000

Then one of the criminals who were hanged blasphemed Him,
saying, "If You are the Christ, save Yourself and us."
But the other, answering, rebuked him, saying,
"Do you not even fear God, seeing you are under the same
condemnation? And we indeed justly, for we receive the due
reward of our deeds; but this Man has done nothing wrong."
Then he said to Jesus, "Lord, remember me
when You come into Your kingdom."
Luke 23:39–42 NKJV

Three wooden crosses stood on the hill that day. Soldiers gathered nearby, gambling to see who would win Christ's garments. Two of the men were thieves who certainly deserved some sort of punishment, but the third figure, the One who claimed to be the Son of God, was blameless.

While hanging on his cross, one thief taunted Jesus; the other thief asked Him for mercy. One thief chose to blaspheme the Son of God while the other chose to worship Him. So the wise thief ended his life that day, but he did not perish. After breathing his last, that man awoke in the arms of the eternal **1**, His Savior.

We know very little about the thief who accepted Christ. We have no details about his life, whether he ever experienced a **3**, or a **12**, or a **120**. But what we do know is this: That man reached out in his last moments here on earth—and he became a powerful example to the world—by achieving the final number of The ManCode: the **3000**. His story has touched the hearts of millions and will continue to echo throughout eternity.

Choices. You must make hundreds of them every day, thousands every week, hundreds of thousands every year. But only one choice will determine your destiny here on earth and your destiny throughout eternity. That choice, simply stated, is this: What will you decide to do about Jesus?

You are free to choose, as one of the thieves did, to say no to Christ. You can choose to mock the Son of God in an overt fashion, or you can choose a more subtle form of mockery by professing to be a Christian with your words but not with your actions. In either event, you'll rob yourself of the abundance and joy that might otherwise be yours in Him. Or, you can make a different choice.

If you choose to say yes to Jesus—completely and without reservation—you'll experience a personal and spiritual transformation. You'll become a different man, a different husband, a different father, and a better servant to the world. When you say yes to Christ, you receive His love and companionship today, tomorrow, and forever. It's a blessing beyond belief and beyond compare.

The choice is yours and yours alone . . .

APPENDIX

1   3   12   120   3000

ABOUT THE HOLY SPIRIT

Jesus promised that He would send a Counselor, a Spirit who would reveal God's truth to His followers:

And I will ask the Father, and he will give you another Counselor, who will never leave you. He is the Holy Spirit, who leads into all truth. The world at large cannot receive him, because it isn't looking for him and doesn't recognize him. But you do, because he lives with you now and later will be in you.
(John 14:16-17 NLT)

The Holy Spirit should be an important topic for all Christians, but it's a topic that lots of folks ignore. So, some of you guys are probably rolling your eyes right about now, thinking that any discussion about the Holy Spirit is either over your head or outside your theology, or both. And although millions of words have been written—and almost as many sermons preached—about the miraculous workings of the Holy Ghost, many men still "tune out" their brains and hearts whenever the subject comes up. In fact, some guys become downright uncomfortable whenever the topic turns to the Spirit with a capital S. But Jesus certainly didn't make that mistake. No, the Master wasn't at all bashful about describing the "Helper" He would send to touch the hearts of His followers and guide their paths. And if the Son of God focused on the Holy Spirit, so should we.

Without the Holy Spirit, that Pentecost miracle, as described in the second chapter of Acts, would never have occurred. After all, the Bible teaches us that it was the Holy Spirit who touched the 120 folks who were gathered together on that fateful day (only ten days after Christ's ascension). And it was the Holy Spirit who gave those 120 believers the ability to speak in many different tongues, thus launching the tremendous growth of the early church. Here's what happened:

> On the day of Pentecost, seven weeks after Jesus' resurrection, the believers were meeting together in one place. Suddenly, there was a sound from heaven like the roaring of a mighty windstorm in the skies above them, and it filled the house where they were meeting. Then, what looked like flames or tongues of fire appeared and settled on each of them. And everyone present was filled with the Holy Spirit and began speaking in other languages, as the Holy Spirit gave them this ability. Godly Jews from many nations were living in Jerusalem at that time. When they heard this sound, they came running to see what it was all about, and they were bewildered to hear their own languages being spoken by the believers. They were beside themselves with wonder. "How can this be?" they exclaimed. "These people are all from Galilee, and yet we hear them speaking the languages of the lands where we were born! Here we are Parthians, Medes, Elamites, people from Mesopotamia, Judea, Cappadocia, Pontus, the province of Asia, Phrygia, Pamphylia, Egypt,

and the areas of Libya toward Cyrene, visitors from Rome (both Jews and converts to Judaism), Cretans, and Arabians. And we all hear these people speaking in our own languages about the wonderful things God has done!"
(Acts 2:1-11 NLT)

The Holy Spirit transformed disciples from closed-door believers into "lion-like men of boldness." The Spirit energized men to such a degree that Peter (the denier) became a bold preacher. And the Holy Spirit still works that way. The Holy Spirit has a strengthening effect that allows believers to stop playing defense and start playing offense. And the Holy Spirit offers comfort in times of hardship.

When God tugs at your heart, the tug you feel is the Holy Spirit! Are you willing to open your heart and let the Spirit in? If so, you'll be forever changed, and your world will be forever changed, too. By welcoming the Spirit into your heart and soul, you'll allow God to work in you and through you. Then, like one of the 120 faithful believers on the day of Pentecost, you'll be destined to change *your* world and *the* world.

Remember: the Holy Spirit plays an integral role in the ways that Christians reach out to the world. In Acts 1:8 Jesus proclaimed, "But you will receive power when the Holy Spirit has come upon you, and you will be My witnesses in Jerusalem, in all Judea and Samaria, and to the ends of the earth" (Holman CSB).

WHAT THE BIBLE SAYS
ABOUT THE HOLY SPIRIT

For our gospel did not come to you in word only, but also in power, and in the Holy Spirit and in much assurance, as you know what kind of men we were among you for your sake.

1 Thessalonians 1:5 NKJV

But when the Holy Spirit controls our lives, he will produce this kind of fruit in us: love, joy, peace, patience, kindness, goodness, faithfulness, gentleness, and self-control. Here there is no conflict with the law.

Galatians 5:22-23 NLT

But when the Helper comes, whom I shall send to you from the Father, the Spirit of truth who proceeds from the Father, He will testify of Me.

John 15:26 NKJV

Now God has revealed them to us by the Spirit, for the Spirit searches everything, even the deep things of God.

1 Corinthians 2:10 Holman CSB

A FEW MORE OBSERVATIONS
ABOUT THE HOLY SPIRIT

We men like to think we are in charge, don't we? But in truth, as much as we posture and strategize, God is truly in control. If only we would yield to what He is doing in our lives.

Steve Cretin

What the church needs is not better machinery nor new organizations, but instead it needs men whom the Holy Spirit can use—men of prayer, men mighty in prayer.

E. M. Bounds

A keen mind and theological training are useful tools when they are sanctified, but the Holy Spirit is our teacher, and He who inspired the Bible is the best interpreter of it.

Vance Havner

The Holy Spirit is no skeptic, and the things he has written in our hearts are not doubts or opinions, but assertions—surer and more certain than sense or life itself.

Martin Luther

THE MANCODE IS
A SELF-DIAGNOSTIC TOOL

If you're experiencing tough times, you can use The ManCode to perform a quick-but-effective way to understand your problems. Here's how to make the diagnosis:

1. First, ask yourself if you have the **1** in your life.

2. Next: Do you have a strong **3** and, just as importantly, are you using them?

3. Next: Are you surrounded by an active, involved **12**?

4. Are you a positive, faithful, contributing member of an enthusiastic **120**?

5. Are you tapping into your **3000** by reaching out to your community and to your world? In other words, are you finding meaningful ways to serve God and share His Good News?

If you've attended to the five numbers of The ManCode, you'll begin to achieve a sense of balance in your life. But if these numbers are not right—if you lack even a single number in The ManCode—you'll need to make things right before you can expect to receive the best things that God has planned for you.

So put all your numbers in place and get ready for God to do important work in you and through you.

――――――――――――――――――――

*God's various gifts are handed out everywhere;
but they all originate in God's Spirit. God's various ministries
are carried out everywhere; but they all originate in
God's Spirit. God's various expressions of power are in action
everywhere; but God himself is behind it all. Each person is
given something to do that shows who God is: Everyone gets in
on it, everyone benefits. All kinds of things are handed out
by the Spirit, and to all kinds of people!*

1 Corinthians 12:4-7 MSG

PERSONAL BIBLE STUDY
AND PROVERBIAL WISDOM

Every man needs the benefit of regular Bible study, so make sure that your 3—and at least some members of your 12—are encouraging you to stay focused on the regular study of God's Word.

When your troubles threaten to make you feel like a living, breathing tackling dummy (and everybody plays the dummy from time to time), the answers you need are as close as the nearest Bible. God's Word doesn't grow old and it doesn't go out of style. And it contains timely, practical instructions for every aspect of your life. So when in doubt, consult your Bible—and a great place to start is in the book of Proverbs.

Proverbs contains 31 chapters. So when you read a chapter a day, you can easily finish the whole book in a month. Then, when the next month rolls around, you can turn back to chapter 1 and start the whole process over again.

When you make Proverbs a regular part of your daily Bible study, you'll weave God's wisdom into the fabric of your day. And you'll start tackling life's problems *before* they tackle you.

_____

A wise man will listen and increase his learning,
and a discerning man will obtain guidance.

Proverbs 1:5 HCSB

CODEKILLERS

In order to implement your own personal Code, you must learn to defeat a dangerous collection of vices we call CodeKillers. CodeKillers are the destructive behaviors, the mistaken attitudes, the bad habits, and the chronically misdirected thought patterns that create distance between you and God. Just about any bad habit you can name has the power to come between you and the Lord, and when it does, the warning bells should start going off in your brain.

We can all think of men who have been destroyed by their own addictions, whether to drugs, to alcohol, to women, or to gambling. And we've all known guys whose inability to grow up (and behave themselves like a real man) caused untold suffering for themselves and their families. Of course, it goes without saying (but we'll say it anyway) that you certainly don't want to find yourself caught up in personal self-destruction like that.

So here's a "Ten Most Wanted List" of CodeKillers that you should watch for and run from. These Killers can wreck your life or, in some cases, even end it. Please be on the alert for these self-destructive tendencies and do whatever it takes to vanquish them. Or else.

1. **Addiction:** If we become addicted to any substance or behavior, the addiction begins to rule our lives—the addiction comes first, ahead of God or just about anything else, for that matter. And whenever we relegate God to

a secondary position in our hearts and minds, we always suffer.

2. Dishonesty: God is truth and He loves truth. Whenever we are dishonest, whether with others or with ourselves, we create a wall—a needless and destructive wall—between ourselves and our Creator.

3. Bitterness: Bitterness focuses on the "unfairness" of the past. But God intends for us to focus on His unimaginable gifts and on the blessings He has in store for us. When we become embittered, we focus too intently on yesterday, and we fail to thank God for His blessings and His love *today.*

4. Greed: When we focus too intently on acquiring money or possessions, the things we're striving to obtain become "substitute gods." And they inevitably separate us from the One true God.

5. Hopelessness: When we abandon hope, we're saying (at least on an unconscious level) that our problems are simply too big for God. And our failure to trust Him leads, not surprisingly, to *even more* helplessness. It's a very dangerous cycle.

6. Impulsiveness: Throughout the Bible, God instructs us to think first and act second (if you don't believe it, try reading a few chapters in Proverbs). So when we *act* first and *think* second, we're disobeying God (and inviting unwelcome consequences as a result).

7. **Irrational Fear:** Some fears are rational, and some fears are not. The irrational kind causes us to become stuck in emotional quicksand. While we're stuck, we cannot become the men God wants us to become.

8. **Immaturity:** Some of us never quite seem to grow up, and in some respects, that's good. After all, it's healthy to retain that childlike sense of wonder and excitement. But not all forms of immaturity are healthy, and when grown men shirk their responsibilities while behaving themselves like irresponsible schoolboys, God isn't pleased . . . and eventually He shows it.

9. **Chronic Anger:** Some men seem to stay angry most of the time. And it's a shame because all that anger leaves little or no room in their hearts for joy, for love, for praise, or for thanksgiving.

10. **Apathy:** Some men seem to give up on life and, without realizing it, on God. Once they've given up, it can be very hard for these fellows to jumpstart their lives. But the good news is this: With God, all things are possible, including life-altering, soul-transforming jumpstarts for apathetic men.

CodeKillers are always destructive, but they are never insurmountable. In fact, the minute you decide to overcome any personal shortcoming, God stands ready to help you succeed. With Him, all things are possible. And if you sincerely ask for His help in the struggle against CodeKillers, He will give it. So ask Him. Now.

———————————

Man without God is always torn between two urges.
His nature prompts him to do wrong,
and his conscience urges him to do right.
Christ can rid you of that inner conflict.

Billy Graham

POWERFUL IDEAS
FOR LIVING WISELY AND WELL

We'll wrap things up with a collection of timely, practical, thought-provoking quotations from noted Christian men. And by the way, if you haven't already done so, you should probably start jotting down some of your own favorite quotations in a place where you can review them often.

ABOUT WISDOM

Knowledge is horizontal.
Wisdom is vertical; it comes down from above.

Billy Graham

The fruit of wisdom is Christlikeness, peace,
humility, and love. And, the root of it is faith in Christ
as the manifested wisdom of God.

J. I. Packer

The more wisdom enters our hearts,
the more we will be able to trust our hearts
in difficult situations.

John Eldredge

The man who prays ceases to be a fool.

Oswald Chambers

If you lack knowledge, go to school.
If you lack wisdom, get on your knees.

Vance Havner

ABOUT THE IMPORTANCE OF MAKING GOOD DECISIONS

Every time you make a choice, you are turning
the central part of you, the part that chooses,
into something a little different from what it was before.

C. S. Lewis

Good and evil both increase at compound interest.
That is why the little decisions you and I make every day
are of such infinite importance.

C. S. Lewis

Every day, I find countless opportunities to decide
whether I will obey God and demonstrate my love for Him
or try to please myself or the world system.
God is waiting for my choices.

Bill Bright

Life is a series of choices between the bad, the good,
and the best. Everything depends on how we choose.

Vance Havner

Successful people make right decisions early
and manage those decisions daily.

John Maxwell

ABOUT NOT GIVING UP

God sometimes permits us to experience humiliating
defeats in order to test our faith and to reveal to us
what's really going on in our hearts.

Warren Wiersbe

You've got problems; I've got problems;
all God's children have got problems. The question is
how are you going to deal with them?

John Maxwell

Life will be made or broken at the place where we meet
and deal with obstacles.

E. Stanley Jones

When you fall and skin your knees and skin your heart,
He'll pick you up.

Charles Stanley

Only the man who follows the command of Jesus
single-mindedly and unresistingly lets his yoke rest upon
him, finds his burden easy, and under its gentle pressure
receives the power to persevere in the right way.

Dietrich Bonhoeffer

ABOUT DOING THE RIGHT THING RIGHT NOW

What you do reveals what you believe about God, regardless of what you say. When God reveals what He has purposed to do, you face a crisis—a decision time. God and the world can tell from your response what you really believe about God.

Henry Blackaby

Discrepancies between values and practices create chaos in a person's life.

John Maxwell

Every time you refuse to face up to life and its problems, you weaken your character.

E. Stanley Jones

Let us not be content to wait and see what will happen, but give us the determination to make the right things happen.

Peter Marshall

Remember that the Christian life is one of action, not of speech and daydreams. Let there be few words and many deeds, and let them be done willingly.

Vincent Pallotti

ABOUT FAMILY

The first essential for a happy home is love.

Billy Graham

A family is a place where principles are hammered
and honed on the anvil of everyday living.

Charles Swindoll

The only true source of meaning in life is found in love
for God and his son Jesus Christ, and love for mankind,
beginning with our own families.

James Dobson

Every Christian family ought to be, as it were,
a little church, consecrated to Christ,
and wholly influenced and governed by His rules.

Jonathan Edwards

The family circle is the supreme conductor
of Christianity.

Henry Drummond

ABOUT THE IMPORTANCE OF SETTING
A GOOD EXAMPLE

In our faith we follow in someone's steps. In our faith we leave footprints to guide others. It's the principle of discipleship.

Max Lucado

If you want your neighbor to know what Christ will do for him, let the neighbor see what Christ has done for you.

Henry Ward Beecher

Nothing speaks louder or more powerfully than a life of integrity.

Charles Swindoll

Our walk counts far more than our talk, always!

George Mueller

A man ought to live so that everybody knows he is a Christian, and most of all, his family ought to know.

D. L. Moody

ABOUT LEADERSHIP

When God wants to accomplish something, He calls dedicated men and women to challenge His people and lead the way.

Warren Wiersbe

People who inspire others are those who see invisible bridges at the end of dead-end streets.

Charles Swindoll

The great illusion of leadership is to think that others can be led out of the desert by someone who has never been there.

Henri Nouwen

A wise leader chooses a variety of gifted individuals. He complements his strengths.

Charles Stanley

You can never separate a leader's actions from his character.

John Maxwell

ABOUT THE NEED TO SERVE

You can judge how far you have risen in the scale
of life by asking one question: How wisely and how deeply
do I care? To be Christianized is to be sensitized.
Christians are people who care.

E. Stanley Jones

In Jesus, the service of God and the service
of the least of the brethren were one.

Dietrich Bonhoeffer

Christianity, in its purest form, is nothing more than
seeing Jesus. Christian service, in its purest form,
is nothing more than imitating him who we see.
To see his Majesty and to imitate him:
that is the sum of Christianity.

Max Lucado

You were created to add to life on earth,
not just take from it.

Rick Warren

Have thy tools ready; God will find thee work.

Charles Kingsley

ABOUT THE NEED TO RECOGNIZE
AND SEIZE OPPORTUNITIES

Never fancy you could be something if only you had
a different lot and sphere assigned to you.
The very things that you most denounce as fatal limitations
or obstructions, are probably what you most want.
What you call hindrances, obstacles, discouragements,
are probably God's opportunities.

Horace Bushnell

Great opportunities often disguise themselves
in small tasks.

Rick Warren

He who waits until circumstances completely favor
his undertaking will never accomplish anything.

Martin Luther

God surrounds you with opportunity.
You and I are free in Jesus Christ, not to do
whatever we want, but to be all that God wants us to be.

Warren Wiersbe

Life is a glorious opportunity.

Billy Graham

ABOUT OPTIMISM

The people whom I have seen succeed best in life have
always been cheerful and hopeful people who went about
their business with a smile on their faces.

Charles Kingsley

It is a remarkable thing that some of the most optimistic
and enthusiastic people you will meet are those
who have been through intense suffering.

Warren Wiersbe

The essence of optimism is that it takes no account of
the present, but it is a source of inspiration, of vitality,
and of hope. Where others have resigned, it enables a man
to hold his head high, to claim the future for himself,
and not abandon it to his enemy.

Dietrich Bonhoeffer

The popular idea of faith is of a certain obstinate optimism:
the hope, tenaciously held in the face of trouble,
that the universe is fundamentally friendly
and things may get better.

J. I. Packer

Great hopes make great men.

Thomas Fuller

ABOUT BEING JOYFUL

A child of God should be a visible beatitude for joy
and a living doxology for gratitude.

C. H. Spurgeon

Joy is the serious business of heaven.

C. S. Lewis

When we get rid of inner conflicts and wrong attitudes
toward life, we will almost automatically burst into joy.

E. Stanley Jones

Joy in life is not the absence of sorrow.
The fact that Jesus could have joy in the midst of sorrow is
proof that we can experience this too.

Warren Wiersbe

The joy of the Holy Spirit is experienced by giving thanks
in all situations.

Bill Bright

ABOUT OVERCOMING WORRY

When the temptation to worry first arrives,
that's the critical moment. The tendency is to invite it
into our thoughts. But worry must be stopped.
We must refuse to invite it into our thoughts.

Charles Swindoll

Worry and anxiety are sand in the machinery of life;
faith is the oil.

E. Stanley Jones

Worry makes you forget who's in charge.

Max Lucado

The secret of Christian quietness is not indifference,
but the knowledge that God is my Father, He loves me,
and that I shall never think of anything He will forget.
Then, worry becomes an impossibility.

Oswald Chambers

God is bigger than your problems.
Whatever worries press upon you today,
put them in God's hands and leave them there.

Billy Graham

ABOUT TRUSTING GOD

Faith is unutterable trust in God,
trust which never dreams that He will not stand by us.

Oswald Chambers

Faith does not eliminate problems.
Faith keeps you in a trusting relationship with God
in the midst of your problems.

Henry Blackaby

Trusting God doesn't change our circumstances.
Perfect trust in Him changes us.

Charles Swindoll

God is God. He knows what he is doing.
When you can't trace his hand, trust his heart.

Max Lucado

Trust in yourself and you are doomed to disappointment;
trust in money and you may have it taken from you,
but trust in God, and you are never to be
confounded in time or eternity.

D. L. Moody

ABOUT GOD'S GRACE

If we only believe and ask,
a full measure of God's grace is available to any of us.

Charles Swindoll

Grace comes from the heart of a gracious God who wants
to stun you and overwhelm you with a gift you don't
deserve—salvation, adoption, a spiritual ability to use in
kingdom service, answered prayer, the church,
His presence, His wisdom, His guidance, His love.

Bill Hybels

We are here to be living monuments to God's grace.

Oswald Chambers

Sin made us poor, but grace makes us rich.

Warren Wiersbe

The cross was heavy, the blood was real, and the price was
extravagant. It would have bankrupted you or me,
so he paid it for us. Call it simple. Call it a gift.
But don't call it easy. Call it what it is. Call it grace.

Max Lucado

ABOUT THE AUTHORS

Dennis Swanberg served the local church in pastoral ministry for 23 years. Then, in 1995, Dennis took a leap of faith when he stepped down as church pastor and stepped up to the microphone. Soon, Swan became "America's Minister of Encouragement," a job he takes seriously as he continues to speak to about 150 churches and organizations every year. He has hosted two successful TV series, authored eight books, and created over a dozen DVDs.

Dennis is a graduate of Baylor University where he majored in both Greek and Religion (1976). He earned both a Master of Divinity (1980) and a Doctor of Ministry (1986) at Southwestern Seminary, Ft. Worth, Texas.

Dennis is married to Lauree Wilkes of Ft. Worth. He has two grown sons: Chad and Dusty. The Swans make their home in Monroe, Louisiana.

Ron Smith is an artist manager, product developer, and business consultant. His clients have included Veggie Tales, Word Music, Random House, Classic Media, and many others. Ron's company has developed more than 400 products for retailers worldwide. And he has managed Dennis Swanberg for more than a decade.

Ron is a graduate of Trevecca Nazarene University and is married to Michelle McSpadden Smith. Together they have three children: Chase, Cole, and Carley. The family resides in Brentwood, Tennessee.

**Discounts available
for bulk orders of 10 books or more.**

Visit

www.TheManCode.net

Or Call

615-790-1118

Coming soon!
The ManCode Workbook and *The ManCode LIVE*—
downloadable video for local interactive events.

Help spread the word!
Encourage your pastor, men's ministry leader,
small group leader, friends and family to download
the FREE sample chapter of *The ManCode!*
www.TheManCode.net